AMERICAN EDUCATION

Its Men

Ideas

and

Institutions

Advisory Editor

Lawrence A. Cremin
Frederick A. P. Barnard Professor of Education
Teachers College, Columbia University

Our Enemy
The Child

Agnes De Lima

ARNO PRESS & THE NEW YORK TIMES
New York * *1969*

Reprint edition 1969 by Arno Press, Inc.

*

Library of Congress Catalog Card No. 78-89172

*

Reprinted from a copy in Teachers College Library

*

Manufactured in the United States of America

Editorial Note

AMERICAN EDUCATION: *Its Men, Institutions and Ideas* presents selected works of thought and scholarship that have long been out of print or otherwise unavailable. Inevitably, such works will include particular ideas and doctrines that have been outmoded or superseded by more recent research. Nevertheless, all retain their place in the literature, having influenced educational thought and practice in their own time and having provided the basis for subsequent scholarship.

Lawrence A. Cremin
Teachers College

Our Enemy
The Child

OUR ENEMY
THE CHILD

By Agnes de Lima

NEW YORK
NEW REPUBLIC, INC.
1926

To SIGRID

AGED THREE AND A HALF,
FROM WHOM I HAVE LEARNED
MORE ABOUT EDUCATION
THAN FROM ANY PEDAGOGUE
OR ANY BOOK

CONTENTS

OUR ENEMY THE CHILD

INTRODUCTION

THE son of a Persian gentleman of old was trained to do three things: to shoot a bow, to ride a horse and to speak the truth. Thus equipped, he was counted educated, prepared to meet the relatively simple requirements of Persian society, a society which required little of its members beyond military prowess, physical vigor and moral integrity. No doubt even then, the pedagogues and wise men indulged in dogma and much argument concerning the training of youth and his ultimate destiny, but the ends of education were at any rate clearly defined and the means for attaining them readily at hand.

Not so, alas, to-day. Go through a recent set of books on education and you will find as many different conceptions of its function as there are writers. Shall the goal be a high degree of intellectual power, or narrow vocational fitness? Shall we stress the individual merely, or his future place in society? Shall the means be rigorous routine or freedom carried to unbelievable lengths? Shall we draw heavily on the classics, the learning of the past, or shall we be guided by science and present-day discoveries? Who knows? Who has the wisdom to answer? Is not one pedagogue's guess as good as another's? It would seem so, for with all their dogma and valiant assertion, none of them appears sure of his ground save when indicting his fellows.

On one thing only are they agreed—the child, the cause of all their adumbrations must be destroyed, or at any rate subdued; and transformed from the alien, independent being he was created, to a creature more pliant to their purposes. The theory of infant damnation still animates too much of our educational policy. Children must be cured of their original sin, have the nonsense knocked out of them, be molded into shape, made fit for society. Unless it is forced upon them by an army of schoolmasters, truant officers and the hands of the law, they will eschew "education" and all of its works.

Recently however there has been a revolt against this cherished tradition. A number of schools are actually daring to put to the test an entirely opposite theory which holds that the natural impulses of the child are creative, that given proper materials and the opportunity to use them, freed from dictation, the child will develop powers and abilities hitherto undreamed of. This does not mean allowing children to "run wild," but rather giving them sufficient content and sufficient opportunity for self-expression fitted to the particular stage of growth they have reached. The old education—or rather the prevailing mode of instruction that is called education—has arbitrarily collected the learning and culture of the past, broken it up into water tight compartments, called "subjects" and arranged these in sequential divisions, running from simple to complex, each logically related to the one preceding. Now as a matter of fact, although we do not know very much about the learning process—innumerable doctors' dissertations on the subject to the contrary—we have at least discovered that it is not a logical affair at all, and that for all our logical pains children do not learn that way. In the experimental classes directed by Miss Irwin, described in Chapter IV, a number of second grade pupils who had not had any arithmetic at all in their first year of schooling, suddenly demanded it. Within a month some of the brighter ones had gone swiftly up to complicated work with fractions without the necessity of memorizing the multiplication tables and the "combinations" which commonly precede such work. Similarly geography in the newer schools is no longer confined to lessons out of a single big book filled with maps and lists of rivers and capitals and products. Youngsters below the kindergarten begin to "get oriented in space." They locate their room in relation to others in the building, they locate the school in relation to other buildings in the street. Later they follow the street to the river, they see the docks, the ferry, the ships. What better impetus could they have to acquire not only geography facts but facts about economics and industry as well? That this theory is sound is shown by the amazing amount of information which the children in these newer schools actually possess. A group of twelve-year-old children of the Walden School who asked Dr. Alexander Goldenweiser to give them a course in anthropology, discussed civilization, the inheritance of acquired characteristics, free will, totem and taboo, social usages, the worth of custom and other matters usually reserved for far maturer classrooms. Yet these children are not intellectual prodigies, they are merely boys and girls whose natural curiosities have not been stifled and whose will-to-think has not been broken.

Now in order to think, one cannot sit passively by and absorb knowledge from the lips of a teacher. A child does not learn to walk by having some grown-up tell him how to do it, by being given a technical description of the motor co-ordination involved in the act. When he is ready to walk, he teaches himself through trial and error, bumps and falls, how to balance and how to propel one foot before the other. And so in these newer schools, every opportunity is given to children to discover things for themselves. One of the most certain ways of achieving this is to provide them plenty of materials with which they can reconstruct and vivify past experiences and thus lay a basis for further inquiry. Nothing indeed more obviously distinguishes the old schools from the new than this use of materials. In the traditional school, the classrooms are a barren waste of desks and blackboards, and materials confined to paper, pencils and books. Even in the kindergarten the materials are limited and their use proscribed. In the newer schools however, the children even up to the highest grades are surrounded with a great variety of things to do with—blocks, paints, crayons, weaving, clay, sand, lumber, boats, printing presses, typewriters, science apparatus, stage sets, sewing machines, electrical appliances, every manner of musical instrument—the list of materials in one descriptive book on experimental practice covers many paragraphs of close type. Books take their rightful place among the materials, as sources of information to supplement first hand experiences, and as rich reference sources.

Now what happens when a child is not dictated to and is set down with materials such as these? If he is emotionally untrammeled and physically sound so that he can function normally, it is safe to say that his use of materials will be creative. Watch a two-year-old piling his blocks. If some adult has not ruined his first efforts by stupidly showing him how, he quite uncannily arranges them in designs having no little degree of balance and proportion. Leave a little child alone with paints or crayons and large sheets of paper and after a period of random smearing, he will begin to draw amazing things, astonishing both in line and color. Even if his products have no meaning for a grown person, they have meaning to him as a child. A three-year-old girl recently showed a visitor a drawing she had made of a man. "Oh," exclaimed the visitor, "what a funny man, he's got only one leg." The child flushed under the criticism, but luckily stood her ground, "Well, that's the kind of man he is!" she replied.

To be sure the newer schools are facing innumerable unsolved problems. Not the least of these is the common human failing of substituting—in the name of freedom—merely another kind of tyranny for the old. Many of the newer institutions tend to regard some sociological or psychological principle as more sacred than the child. In many it is the great abstraction of the future society which is set above every other consideration; the curriculum is "socialized," all efforts are bent to making the child an intelligent participant in a future social democracy. To this end, the pupil is given endless material bearing on the mechanics of modern industry and government—a sort of glorified civics—calculated to turn him into a kind of socialized robot who will infallibly coöperate smoothly and efficiently with his fellows. Other advocates of "freedom" are busy instilling habits in mere toddlers and runabouts, habits which may or may not limit spontaneity, independence and initiative. Others are magnifying the bogey of "emotional fixation" and "complexes" to absurd proportions. Some of these dangers are specifically referred to in the present discussion.

While these shortcomings are serious and may become more so as experimental schools multiply in number, the great battle is still to be won for even a modicum of free activity in the ordinary school. While informality in the classroom is on the increase the great majority of children are still being made the victims of a repressive régime too much like the one described in the first chapters. Few public schools have advanced as far as such conservative demonstration schools as the Horace Mann and Ethical Culture Schools, which are described in Chapter IX. The valuable contributions to scientific curriculum making worked out by the Lincoln School have scarcely been heard of by the rank and file of teachers throughout the country. The Gary and Dalton schools are making headway but with painful slowness, considering how easily they may be adapted to public school conditions. In only a few instances have public school classes been established—and they are usually short lived—which experiment radically along the lines suggested by such institutions as the City and Country, and the Walden Schools in New York City.

Yet there is a stirring in the educational world. Everywhere there is evidence of a profound and growing dissatisfaction with the existing educational order. When Mr. Israel Zangwill announced that America is the best half educated nation in the world, his remarks were greeted with a chorus of approval. Knocking our schools and the products of our schools will "get a hand" not only from the gallery of disgruntled proletarians, but from the center of the house made up of solid business men, professional workers and the saving remnant of the blue stocking clan.

Most thoughtful teachers have felt the force of public school criticism for years. Many have resisted inwardly, but have felt that open revolt was futile. Others have attempted change, but lacking the necessary technique or scientific knowledge or sufficient imagination have slipped back into old ways, because old ways are easy and safe and well known. To-day, however, there exists not only a growing store of scientific information and of pedagogical discovery, but the centers, both public and private where the newer educational theories are being put to the test, are growing in number and influence. The Teachers' Union in New York City has prepared an ambitious proposal for establishing such an experiment station within the public school system itself. Over a thousand public school teachers in the metropolis belong to a society for the experimental study of education. The sessions of this organization, while still confined too narrowly to technical problems of measurement, or of pedagogy, are increasingly devoted to consideration of more fundamental educational reform. Schools of education of universities and research bureaus in city school systems, while by no means committed to the liberalizing principles of the more radical experimental centers, are giving them thoughtful attention. Moreover the lay public is showing a growing interest in educational progress. The Progressive Education Association has begun the publication of a notable laymen's quarterly, whose gifted editor is Miss Gertrude Hartman. Finally, organized labor, originally responsible for the first great educational experiment—the establishment for the first time anywhere of a system of free and universal education,—is again taking a hand in educational reform. Not only has labor taken vigorous steps to improve and expand the range of educational opportunities for adults, but more recently working people, both organized and unorganized, have taken an aggressive attitude in regard to elementary instruction. This attitude has been the more significant, because it has been concerned not with questions of extending the school age, or the school year, nor with matters relating to narrow vocational training. Labor is actually putting the question, "What opportunities are the schools giving our children to become free creative personalities?" This question appears to the workingman to be of supreme importance, for without a generation of free and creative individuals, the ends and aims of the organized labor movement can never be achieved.

The author of the present volume has spent many years visiting and "surveying" schools of the traditional type. More recently she devoted a year to studying the specific experiments described in these pages. Chapters II, III and XII appeared as articles in the *New Republic*, and parts of others were published in the *New Republic* and the *Nation*. Thanks are therefore due to the editors of these magazines for permission to reprint this material.

II

A SCHOOL MORNING

"Sɪᴛ up tall—every one of you!" commanded the teacher.

Forty-six boys, ranging in age from nine to twelve, their arms crossed behind them, chests swelled to bursting, strained themselves against the backs of their desks.

The teacher regarded them fixedly until the last child was frozen into immobility.

"Arithmetic books—out!" At the signal, forty-six books appeared on the desks.

"Begin at the top of page 47 and work examples 12, 13, 14 and 15. All except you, Nathan, and you, Davis, and you, Paul. You three go to the board and write down what I tell you."

"These dull fellows need a little extra drill," declared the teacher in a loud aside to the visitor. "I always say the dull child has as much right to be educated as the smart one. That means giving him a hand once in a while. Now then, boys, clear the board. Put down six million, three hundred and twenty-seven thousand, five hundred and forty-two. Divide by nine hundred and fifteen. Nathan, where are your eyes?"

The teacher's voice was hard and metallic and her face lined with a multitude of little seams of nervous irritation. Police duty is hard work, when it means keeping forty-six children caged and immovable in a tiny room five hours a day, five days a week for ten months a year.

For caged and immovable they were in a space measuring certainly not more than fifteen by thirty feet, a space completely filled by cumbersome desks at which the children sat, two and often three to a seat. Blackboards filled the front and one side wall, a clothes closet ran across the rear, and windows were on the remaining side. A few stereotyped drawings of birds labeled "Bird Week" were pinned to the closet doors and three posters, one of a truck, one of a street car and the third of an ambulance, all marked "Safety First!" surmounted a blackboard. In one corner hung a chart showing liquid measure. Next to it was a small supply chest. On the teacher's desk drooped three peonies at the point of disintegration. On the board in neat script were the letters p-e-o-n-y.

This was actually all there was in the room. In this cramped and arid space was not one thing to call forth the slightest creative impulse of the children who were doomed by law to spend the sunniest hours of their lives there. All they could do was to sit up rigid and "tall," while the teacher doled out irrelevant and uninviting bits of knowledge in the name of "education."

The worst of it was that four years of this kind of treatment had had its deadly effect on the children. They sat there, this spring morning, sunk in apathy, not one of them by even so much as a shuffle venturing to rebel openly against the accustomed régime. One boy, to be sure, instead of working his sums, was, under cover of his hand, scribbling a series of ciphers across his paper, and another was stealthily watching the meaningless performance in awed fascination. The three "dullards" at the board went through the drill with perfect precision. It was without doubt as good a way of passing the time as any other.

At the end of a quarter of an hour the teacher ordered the arithmetic papers to be collected and then announced with a show of liveliness that the class would write a composition about a trip to Central Park planned for the morrow.

The children brightened visibly. Here was a real event worth discussing. They waited cautiously however for directions as to how to proceed to discuss it. The teacher wrote the heading on the board:

"A trip to Central Park."

"Put that down," she commanded. Forty-six pencils wrote as a unit. Then the children waited again.

"Next, write in your own words all the things Miss Perkins has told you not to do on that trip." Not a child moved.

"Oh, come," urged Miss Perkins, "you remember what those things are. Tell us one, Nathan."

"Not to knock no papers on the floor."

"You mean, to throw no papers on the grass. Yes, we must leave everything orderly. What else, Benjamin?"

"Please, we should listen on your whistle and come right back."

"Yes, nobody is to go beyond the sound of my whistle, and the moment I blow it, you must return instantly."

It was no doubt natural that Miss Perkins should be concerned at the prospect of conducting forty-six East Side youngsters to Central Park and back. All but one, she explained, had never been there in their lives, and all but three had never ridden in a street car before. Small wonder that she suggested a composition full of prohibitions.

After a sufficient number of these negative reminders had been given, the children set about writing them down. The task seemed more congenial than the previous one. To discuss a real coming event, even in the negative, was far more agreeable to the children than to work arithmetic sums in vacuo.

The writing period was soon over, however, and the readers were ordered out.

"Turn to page 62," commanded Miss Perkins, "and read, sentence about."

The class relapsed into its former apathy. It had apparently read the story of "Iduna and the Golden Apples" many times before, and the theme was worn threadbare. The children rose mechanically and read the sentences in shrill, labored tones, chopping off each word with meaningless emphasis. A number yawned and squirmed miserably.

Miss Perkins seemed as aware as any one else of the futility of the performance. Still, was she not as trapped as the children? Her time table called for so many minutes of reading daily and the course of study prescribed this particular reader. She must drive relentlessly ahead, in appearance only more free than the driven. She scanned her watch nervously.

"Time for music," she announced.

The class shuffled the readers out of sight and sat woodenly erect.

"Sit up tall," Miss Perkins said for the twentieth time that morning. "Make your mouths nice and round." She drew a little pipe from her pocket and blew "A."

"La-a, everybody!" Her right arm wagged through the air.

The class rose to its feet.

"Now then—'Happy School Days.' Sing as if you meant it. Wake up, can't you? Some of you look only half alive. Remember, we must sing our best on Commencement Day."

Even so, the song dragged miserably.

"We'll try, 'Watchman, What of the Night?' next." The children responded drearily.

"Ready, sit!" ordered Miss Perkins. The class sat.

"Patrick, let us hear you recite, 'Robert of Lincoln.' "

Patrick, a wan, gaunt lad with tousled hair and a splotched face, came up front. He went through the poem at a tremendous speed, intensely eager to get the business over with.

"Peter, recite the same poem. Try to give it a little more expression."

Peter's notion of "expression" was to recite extremely slowly with special emphasis upon the lines, "Bobolink, bobolink, spink, spank, spink."

"Now, everybody, the poem over again."

The class repeated the poem in utter indifference.

"Next, 'The Mountain and the Squirrel,' John!" Miss Perkins moved to the side of the room. Half a dozen heads turned towards her.

"All those facing the side of the room, face front!" she ordered peremptorily. "Go on, John."

"One more—'The Fountain'—Thomas."

Thomas, thin and undersized, one eye twitching nervously, shrieked the verses in his tense treble. The contrast was cruel between his misshapen little frame and the words of the poem. "In-to the sun-shine full of delight . . ." he halted miserably.

"Go ahead," prodded Miss Perkins. Thomas stood his ground a moment in a desperate search for the next line, then crumpled into his place.

"Next boy!" "Next boy" began the poem at the beginning and ran it through successfully.

"Monitors, open the windows!"

A two-minute drill followed, the children responding with exact military precision to the orders given. Every iota of expression had left their faces. Blankly, almost blindly they wheeled from left to right and from right back to left.

They seemed in no wise like children but like wooden dolls moved by a master hand.

"Chests up—in—out! Arms upward stretch —higher—down! Knees—bend! Left—turn— step! Form lines for marching. About face! Mark time—halt! Forward march—halt! Run in place—halt! Forward march—halt! Breathe in—out! Left—turn—to your places, step! Sit!"

The class sat.

Miss Perkins examined them critically "Now that we are all freshened up and have our wits about us, let us try . . . the boys who have pens in their hands, put them down instantly! . . . let us try a spelling match."

This was obviously for the visitor's benefit. The children smiled feebly. "Henry, choose for one side; Patrick, for the other. Be quick."

The spelling match was executed without the slightest show of animation. The class seemed past any possibility of life. But as the big noon bell cut through the building, a shiver of expectancy went over the room. The door opened and a child entered with a note for Miss Perkins. Instantly a score of heads craned down the hall and one boy involuntarily thrust his foot into the aisle . . . in the direction of freedom.

"John!" snapped Miss Perkins, "you may stay

after class for fifteen minutes." She began to count slowly, the signal for the children to get their wraps. Each row rose in turn, faced about and marched in dead silence to the clothes closet, got their wraps and returned to their seats. The other rows waited in an agony of suspense. When every one had hats and coats, Miss Perkins gave the signal to rise. All, save the luckless John, fell into line and marched to the door.

"We shall stand here until every head is still," announced Miss Perkins. "The boy who has his elbows up, put them down." There was another half minute of anguished immobility. "Good morning, boys," said Miss Perkins finally.

"Good morning, Miss Perkins!" came the reply in a roar of spontaneity, the only sincere response of the morning.

Miss Perkins watched the line file down the hall where it was met by other lines, each presided over by its glaring guardian. Only at the downstairs door was vigilance relaxed, when the children burst out into the free air of the streets like so many exploding shells.[1]

[1] The foregoing is an exact transmission of what took place during a visit to a fourth grade class in a New York public school last spring. Both school and class were selected at random, the visitor merely choosing the first school she happened to come across after going into an unfamiliar part of town.

III

THE "BEST" OF SCHOOL MORNINGS[1]

To begin with, Mrs. Spencer was warm and human. She loved her work, she loved the children. You could tell that at once from the way she was addressing the new little boy from Ohio, putting him at his ease, wording the question in

[1] In the present instance an attempt has been made to report the "best" of ordinary school mornings—experimental classes excepted. The principal of the school visited is one of the most enlightened and progressive men in the New York system. His school and his methods have received frequent and well deserved public commendation. The writer asked and received permission to spend the morning with his very best teacher of a fourth grade.

There may be better "best" teachers in the system, but it is worth while to ask just how much in the way of creative experience can be afforded to children by any teacher, no matter how technically skilled or graciously human, who suffers under a fixed course of study, an overcrowded class, a room void of any materials save blackboards, desks and books, and the tradition of the teacher as the active, directing agent, and of the pupils as the docile and receptive ones.

That the class teachers themselves are aware of the difficulties of the job is shown by the remarkable response to the recent request of Supt. Wm. J. O'Shea of New York City that they indicate changes needed in the course of study and in methods of instruction. That they are more aware of the necessity for change than are their superiors is plain from the returns from one district, whose superintendent turned in more than 500 changes suggested by his teachers, only two of which had his endorsement.

denominate numbers with just the right note of apology in her tone so that he might not think New York was talking down to him.

And the children loved her. They were willing in their responses, even the "Pest," a well grown lad of nine who sat right under Mrs. Spencer's desk, and did extremely well under the circumstances.

The circumstances of course were the necessity of sitting as docilely as possible in one seat for hours at a time and letting Mrs. Spencer assign the work, and not only assign it, but for the most part do all the talking about it and all the deciding as to when one job should end and another begin.

To be sure, she did it all in the friendliest way imaginable, with a good deal of understanding of the willingness of children to coöperate in almost any enterprise if only you assume that they will.

The room itself was friendly, large and sunny, with big windows to the rear and the left, giving one a wide expanse of sky and a spreading city below. If forty-two active, restless boys and girls must perforce sit quietly by the hour and listen to abstractions, they could scarce have chosen a more cheerful place. There were flowering plants in boxes at the windows, and the lower sashes of the windows were gay with silhouette drawings made by the children. The same gay frieze of birds and black cats ran over the clothes closet whose doors were covered with a quantity of little prints and placards: "factors," "units," "numerator," "denominator," "mixed number." On the supply closet doors were the Declaration of Independence, a lengthy notice in fine print from the American Legion, concerning Our Flag—How to Display It; How to Respect It, and the roll of local members of the American Junior Red Cross. On a blackboard was written, "I shall pass through this world but once. Any *good* thing therefore that I can do, or any kindness that I can show to any human being, let me do it *now*. Let me not defer it, nor neglect it, for I shall not pass this way again." Over the front board was another placard, "Self Control."

This was evidently the class slogan, for every now and again Mrs. Spencer would pause and point to it half humorously, "Up nice and straight and tall, everybody," her voice would be ever so good-natured, "and let's all of us exercise—"

"Self-control!" the class would answer with equal good humor.

An arithmetic lesson was beginning as we entered. Mrs. Spencer turned from the Ohio boy to a little miss who sat staring at her finished sum with lines of deep worry in her face.

"Good for you, Helen. That's just right—

you didn't know you were so smart." Helen's look of worry dissolved into a smile.

"Little helpers to the board," Mrs. Spencer announced, "George, Edith, Fred, Gertrude, each take two children who need helping." A dozen children ranged themselves around the room grouped in threes. "Begin at page 101 in your books, and start with the first example. You others in your seats, begin at page 115, example 4. Yes, you may talk to one another about your work." A little buzz ran over the room.

There were two grades in the class, Mrs. Spencer explained to the visitor, fifteen bright children from 4a and twenty-seven dull ones from 4b. Both groups were now ready to enter 5a, the bright pupils having done two terms' work in one. Mrs. Spencer was using these bright children as coaches for the slower ones. The plan worked admirably, and gave her a chance to pay more individual attention to those not being coached. It was impossible to give much individual help when one had forty-two children at once. Many of them were serious problems, sent to her because she knew how to deal with them. She never nagged, but tried instead to understand what lay behind a child's behavior.

She consulted her watch. "The coaching period is over," she announced. "To your seats."

"There is one example we all need to talk about," she said, as the children settled themselves. "Thirty-seven and one-half minus twenty-five and one-fifth." She wrote it on the board. "Who can give me the least common denominator? Fanny? I called on you because you weren't paying attention. Well, then, Sam, you tell us. Ten, that's right. Now then, Sam, what do we—oh, I hope you know it—what do we do next?" But Sam stood helplessly at sea. A girl suggested the next step.

"Oh, dear," sighed Mrs. Spencer, "there's a girl here named Sam." But for all the help proffered, Sam was unable to complete the sum without prodigious prodding.

"The arithmetic period is over. Keep your papers in your books. Your homework is example 2 on page 114: 117,799 divided by 3,648. How do we prove an example in division? We mult——"

"Multiply the divisor by the quotient," said the class in unison.

"We are smart to-day. Stephen, what seems to be the trouble?"

Stephen, the "Pest," jerked his head back at the girl behind him. "She keeps sticking her feet into my back," he complained.

"Oh, dear, how dreadful! Such little tiny

feet going right through a big thick bench right into your big strong back! I suppose you are too seriously hurt to go to Mr. Hazen's room and fetch me the map of Asia. You're not? Well, and you, David, go and get the map of Europe from Miss Flynn." Both boys had reached the door as though shot from a gun. "Remember to say 'Please.'" Mrs. Spencer turned to the class. "Always be——"

"Polite," they responded.

"Yes, always be polite, it's worth while, you'll find. Up tall—stretch up—deep breath—out—that's better. While we're waiting for the maps, I want Sarah, George, Walter and Dominick to come up front and recite each a verse of 'Woodman, Spare That Tree!'"

The children ran through the poem with no particular circumstance, save for Sarah, a heavy fat girl who intoned the third stanza with deep emotion.

"Sarah, you were just wonderful!" applauded Mrs. Spencer. "You recited with so much expression, it made my heart go pitta-pat.

"Take out your geographies, and turn to the map of Asia. Page 185.

"Henry, what is Asia?"

"Asia—Asia—" stammered the uncertain Henry.

"Class?"

"Asia is a continent."

"Well, what is the meaning of continent, Elsie?"

"A continent is the largest division of land."

"Right, when I talk about a continent, what do I mean? I mean land."

Stephen returned with the map of Asia and swung it deftly into place over the board. He lingered over the job of straightening it, hating to relinquish even so slight an activity for the detestable business of sitting still. One wondered how much he would have been regarded as a "Pest" if he might have ranged at will through a science laboratory, or spent his excess energies in a school carpentry shop or printing room instead of spending hours at a desk.

"Thank you, Stephen, it looks fine. Take the pointer, and show us the coast-line. Not so fast. What do I mean by coast-line? Right. And from the kind of coast-line that Asia has, what do you think Asia is good for? I'll ask Edna to answer me. To your seat, Stephen."

The questions ran on with their perfunctory answers. "Tell me what you can about the extreme northern part. The coldest part of the world. Right. What about this," pointing to the Tropic of Cancer. "Cold," said one child,

"Hot," said another. "Who said 'Hot'? He was right. Point to the Ural Mountains." Three children tried it in vain. For all Mrs. Spencer's warmth and zeal, the class could not find Asia interesting.

"Hang Asia over the back board and we'll review Europe." At least six boys leaped from their seats to remove the map of Asia and hang Europe in its place.

"I want the Caucasian Mountains, I want the Bay of Biscay. Name five countries of Europe. . . ." But even Europe in review had no attractions. Mrs. Spencer looked at her watch again.

"Why, it's way past time for crackers and milk." A dozen hands waved wildly. Two boys were selected to fetch the milk.

"While we're waiting, who can tell me the name of that pretty little picture over there?" Mrs. Spencer indicated a print. 'Dance of the Nymphs.' Right, Sarah."

"Who remembers the artist?" She wrote Corot on the board.

"What hour of the day is usually depicted in his pictures? Early morning or twilight. And what is there about Corot's pictures that makes them great? Every great artist, children, has something about his pictures that makes them great. And Corot's is what?"

"He leaves something to your imagination," declared Sarah.

"Right," affirmed Mrs. Spencer. "Now, we have only five minutes for crackers and milk.

"We'll have to hurry," Mrs. Spencer appeared to regret the end of recess as much as any one, "but it's time for writing. Monitors pass the papers. Every one up, nice and straight and tall, and do your very best. Write your names. Don't forget to end with an upward stroke. Two or three forgot about the upward stroke last time. It's just as bad as coming to school with your clothes unbuttoned or your necktie off. Write these words."

She wrote a number of words on the board: mountain, camp, August, glove, song, thumb, itself.

"Do your very best. We have only a week or two more before promotion day." A shiver ran over the class. Two or three girls covered their faces with their hands.

Mrs. Spencer erased the words. "Who can spell August? John?"

"August: A-u-g-u-s-t, August," said John quickly.

"What was wrong? Dora?"

"August: *capital* A-u-g-u-s-t, August," declared Dora.

"Right. Time for reading. And we are going to exchange readers with Miss Flynn's class." There were little murmurs of delight. "So we shan't use our own readers to-day, but instead, let's act out one of the stories. Let's do the Mad Tea Party. Who remembers it best?" Four children were chosen.

The playlet went off admirably, the little girl who impersonated Alice, looking exactly like her.

"Fine. You were all good," Mrs. Spencer declared. "Now we'll have a language game. Why do we have language games?"

Nobody appeared to know. "To teach us to speak correct English," said Mrs. Spencer, "always know the reason, children, for what you do. Now I shan't select anybody who isn't sitting up very nice and tall and straight. And look here, young man, when I need any assistance from you I'll ask for it. Too many feet sticking out in this aisle. Under your desks. That's right. We'll play the 'It Is I' game. Edna, you may choose."

All the children hid their faces in their hands, while Edna flew down the aisle, touching this one and that. The "Pest" squirmed miserably.

Another child called the names. As each child was called, he rose and answered, "No, it was not I whom the Fairy touched," or "Yes" as the case might be. The "Pest" extended his arms in utter disgust.

"Stephen," Mrs. Spencer was quite amicable, "I need change for three dollars in dimes to settle our arrangements for seeing Peter Pan. You just run to your father's store and get them for me." Stephen immediately straightened up and left the room with an air of solemn responsibility.

"We'll have a drill game on the word bring," Mrs. Spencer told the class.

The game ended the morning. The children sat passively enough as the successive gongs sounded. They were well-trained and they knew that Mrs. Spencer wanted things to go through in order.

"We'll have the girls choose the best looking boy to escort our visitor back to the principal's office," said Mrs. Spencer. "And we hope she has enjoyed her morning."

IV

SOME SCHOOLS ARE DIFFERENT

I

ACCORDING to a widely current doctrine, there is and must always be a division of labor between the public and the private schools. The private school may undertake extended experiments. It is free, within wide limits to teach such subjects as seem promising, by such methods as appear hopeful. The public school, being essentially bureaucratic, may adopt only the subjects and methods that seem to have a virtual certainty of success. The function of the private school, according to this view, is to probe all things. That of the public school is to hold fast that which is good, or if not good, at least generally acceptable.

There is much justice in these observations. Yet it will not do to press too far the distinction between private and public school. The former is not so free nor the latter so bureaucratic as we usually assume. The public schools, in spite

32

of the handicaps of inadequate staff, congested buildings, political interference, do occasionally respond to the spirit of educational progress. In New York City, where these handicaps are naturally more serious than in smaller cities we nevertheless find significant educational experiments, partly under direct official supervision and guidance, and partly with the encouragement and approval of the supervisory staff. These experiments range in thoroughness from mere regrading and regrouping of children to radical departures from that most sacred of all school traditions—the course of study.

One of the most remarkable of educational experiments is now being carried through by Miss Elisabeth Irwin, under joint public and private auspices. Miss Irwin herself is employed by the Public Education Association, but her staff, except the teacher of music, are public school teachers, and the classes are officially a part of Public School 61, and under the supervision of the Department of Education. Dr. George M. Parker of the Psychiatrist Research Foundation and three associates are also connected with the experiment.

The work started February, 1923, with one hundred children who had attended school for one term. They are now ending their third year and their number will be augmented each term by another group of beginners. It is Miss Irwin's hope to carry these children up to the junior high school, adding new children to fill the lower grades each term. Her classes are of three types: bright, normal, and dull-normal. A class for neurotic children was dropped after the second year. Mental defectives are excluded, since they are already fairly well provided for in the public schools. Preliminary psychological and psychiatric examinations determine in what class each child enters. He is later shifted from one group to another as his needs require.

Except for the normal class, Miss Irwin has greatly reduced the scope of formal work in the three R's. It is her belief that children at this age—between six and nine—require physical exercise, a chance to develop the larger muscles, sensory training in the free use of appropriate materials, clay, wood, sand, color, weaving, plants and the like. She has got rid of immovable school desks, blackboards, etc. In the beginners' room she has provided little wicker easy chairs, tables suited to small statures, work-benches, a typewriter, low shelves containing playthings, flowers, and even a miniature zoo.

This intimate and natural atmosphere is in Miss Irwin's opinion a first requisite in education. The child, she says enters school from an intensely personal background. Everything up to that time has been done in response to appeals from "mamma" or "papa." At the age of six or seven he dashes into a great public building with two or three thousand other children. "He is fitted into a slit between a bench and a desk in a room with fifty others. He must stand up and sit down with them upon command. He learns to shout in chorus certain responses to certain symbols on the blackboard. . . . When a bell rings he goes in; when two bells ring, he goes out. If the bells ring long and loud and unexpectedly, he soon learns that that is a fire-drill and everybody hurries out on the street and the principal shouts things to the teacher. So this is school . . ." [1]

In contrast, Miss Irwin's classrooms are places where children are given an opportunity to gain experience at first hand, freely and naturally. There is no need she thinks of hurrying along the teaching of symbols. Any normal child will learn to read before he is ten, if he is exposed to books by those who value them. There is no use torturing an imaginative child of six or seven with a dull reading routine. No child, however, is too young to begin the study of literature.

[1] "Personal Education," by Elisabeth Irwin, *The New Republic*, Educational Section, Nov. 12, 1924.

"Mother Goose rhymes, folk tales, stories of every day life begin to interest a child during his second year and from then on he will take all he can get. Because he is not taught reading at an early age is no reason to skimp his fund of imaginative material." [2] Similarly with writing. In Miss Irwin's opinion, which she holds in common with many other educators and psychologists, nothing is gained and very much is lost by insistence on the child's learning to write at an early age. No child under eight should be expected to form letters less than a foot high, and even then no high standard of perfection should be imposed. The nerve strain is too severe.

Yet as they become necessary, the three R's are adequately learned. Miss Irwin tells a story of a mother who was distressed because her seven years old George could not write, although he had been in school a term and a half. The family was about to move uptown, and the mother feared for George's standing in a traditional school. "Never mind, we'll teach him to write before you move," Miss Irwin assured her. "But we go next Monday," moaned the mother. "We'll teach him," Miss Irwin repeated. And they did

[2] "Fitting the School to the Child," by Elisabeth Irwin and Louis Marks, The Macmillan Company, 1924.

—in two days! Mrs. Marietta Johnson has spoken of children's "bursting into literacy." Something of the sort happened to this boy.

The daily program in Miss Irwin's rooms bears little resemblance to that of the traditional school. There is none of that quick regimentation of children into docile, silent rows a few moments after the morning bell has sounded. It is to be doubted whether Miss Irwin's children ever conventionally "settle down." In a recent article she has described how they come together in the morning. They enter the room naturally and easily. One child may run up to inspect the fish and superintend their breakfast; another may lovingly linger over his loom and the small rug in process of weaving; a half dozen with no suggestion from the teacher begin to arrange chairs in a semicircle. The children talk as they come together. Five minutes, ten minutes pass. The teacher appears quite unperturbed. She could of course, by a clap of her hands, call the class to order and save these passing minutes. But save them for what? For her own, or the children's purposes?

"After all a child's life is made of time. One of the realities the modern school has to accept is that a child's tempo is different from an adult's. Too much speeding up is a violation of the principle of growth. Therefore tempering the pace of a child's day to his rate of movement is a necessity for which one must sacrifice the number of activities he can undertake." [3]

But finally, in ten minutes or so—to return to the first period of the day—the children are seated, and "Oral English" begins. Or rather the youngsters begin to talk things over.

Miss Irwin places great emphasis on the value to the child of learning to talk. She repudiates utterly the traditional rule, "children should be seen, not heard." The taboo on children's talking in the conventional class room has worked so injuriously that "even when they are released to the playground, their communication with one another consists almost entirely of nudges, shouts and monosyllables." Miss Irwin's children discuss neighborhood and family events, personal exploits or failures, what they saw at their last expedition to the Museum or to the docks. The group sits about informally, discussing naturally as any group will do. There is none of that painful silence which marks so many attempts at class room conversation when a child, at a signal from the teacher, rises awkwardly, says something in a stereotyped fashion and then hastily sits down.

Following the discussion period, there may be an hour of work in reading or arithmetic,

[3] *New Republic,* Nov. 12, 1924.

since the gifted children demand these subjects—largely because of pressure on the part of their parents. After that comes a half hour of music, dancing, rhythm, simple instruments and then play. The afternoon is devoted entirely to free activities. Children may choose to read, to write, to work with hammer, typewriter, weaving, painting, blocks, to run errands on behalf of some class activity, go on expeditions, and the like.

Each class has its own "project" about which most of its group activities center. Once a week one class entertains the rest by an assembly period devoted to their particular project. The children plan and execute the entire performance. The projects selected for one term were Indians by the gifted group, a store by the normal, short plays by the dull, and a circus by the neurotic class. The Indians dressed in costume, and constructed a large wigwam, a real tom-tom, and other Indian paraphernalia fashioned after models in the Museum. They made Indian books and entered in them notes on Indian lore and custom.

Academic work has only recently been begun by the dull class, but the emphasis is placed upon dramatic exercises, upon music and work with materials, color, drawing, shellacking, etc. The principle underlying Miss Irwin's work with the dull group is that ordinary academic training for such children limits rather than helps them. It pushes them into classes "where they are destined always to be at the tail end . . . If we were to analyze 1,000 school children who are social and educational misfits, the great majority of them would certainly be found to belong to this group. The truants, the hold-overs, the disciplinary cases are preponderantly of the dull-normal type." [4] Miss Irwin does not despair of children of this sort. Given an appropriate training, there is a great variety of useful and agreeable occupations open to them. To try instead to force them through a training for which they are not fitted is to inflict signal injury upon them.

The neurotic class was conducted on the assumption that naughtiness and misbehavior are therapeutic rather than moral problems. These children were made the subject of special care and treatment by Dr. Parker and his associates, who gave advice as to both their school and extra-school activities.

The class for neurotic children was important not only because it attempted to salvage lives that would otherwise be thwarted and socially wasted, but also because of the light the work shed on the education of normal children. Much has been

[4] "Fitting the School to the Child," by Elisabeth Irwin and Louis Marks, The Macmillan Company 1924.

learned about the intelligence of normal children from watching the training of those mentally defective. Similarly, much may be discovered about normal emotional development through work with children suffering from neuroses and fears. "We have learned from the neurotic child," Miss Irwin says, "to what a startling degree the emotional status of an individual conditions his future functioning. Yet the school throughout its history has ignored the feeling life of the individual as something outside its province. . . . Perhaps the great hope of the future of education lies in the fact that so far as we know the emotional life of the individual may be infinitely educated." [5]

It is perhaps too early to draw definite conclusions from Miss Irwin's experiment. Even as regards achievement in the formal school subjects, the experiment should not be subjected to comparison with traditional classes, since few achievement tests are valid under the fourth grade. Years of work must be done before we can know certainly what kind of training best fits each group, or even how permanent the group limits are. We cannot doubt however that Miss Irwin is on the track of an educational reform of immense importance. How free a hand she will be

[5] See note, p. 40.

given by the public authorities to develop the
experiment still remains to be seen. How many
other classes similar in organization will be permitted in other sections of the city is also an
open question. The physical difficulties, the large
classes, the lack of money are not the barriers
that stand in the way. The real obstacles are
in the minds of certain of the supervising staff.
"They do not believe," writes Miss Irwin, "that
the physical and emotional demands of children
are valid. And so the schools grind on, impart-
ing information, instilling morals and preparing
children for a future life." [6]

II

Equally radical experiments with public school
classes have been made for a number of years
by Professor Ellsworth Collings, now of the
University of Oklahoma. The first of Professor
Collings' experiments was conducted by him for
four years in a rural elementary school in Mont-
gomery County, Missouri, and has been described
by him in his book, "An Experiment with a
Project Curriculum" (The Macmillan Company).
At present he is experimenting with junior high
school classes in the practice school of the depart-

[6] *New Republic,* Nov. 12, 1924.

ment of education of the University of Oklahoma.

In both experiments, Professor Collings completely abandoned the usual educational aims and methods. His concern is not to teach subjects nor to be guided by any course of study. His aim is to help boys and girls to pursue their own activities better and more fruitfully. The content of the school activities is made up of these interests, the curriculum being constantly made "on the spot" by pupil and teacher in conference. Concretely, the children engage in innumerable enterprises, which fall naturally into four groups: play, excursion, story and hand projects (in the more recent experiment a fifth group has been added,—skill projects). These projects include games, folk dancing, dramatizations, and social parties; studies of community activities and problems; stories in all their forms, oral, song, pictures and music; shop and construction work, making furniture, growing vegetables, preparing school luncheons.

In Missouri, Professor Collings kept current check of the proficiency gained in formal subjects in the experimental school, as well as in two schools following the traditional course of study. The tests at the end of four years showed the experimental school far in the lead. Not only did the children master the three R's more thoroughly, but there were other gains as well. Enrollment and attendance rose to a point well nigh perfect; tardiness and punishment dropped to practically zero, high school entrants increased, while in all these respects the traditional schools maintained their former low level. Moreover the experimental school reacted favorably on the community. More and better periodicals, more and better books found their way into the homes, farm and home conveniences were installed, illness from preventable diseases decreased. As Professor Kilpatrick points out in his introduction to the book, "It can no longer be said that the theory won't work. It has worked. A régime of child purposing is feasible. We can lay aside school subjects as such and succeed—and succeed admirably."

The present experiment of Professor Collings is being carried on with sixty junior high school pupils, twenty in each of the three years. The students are classified on the basis of their I.Q., school achievement and physical development. Five rooms are provided, each equipped not for a given subject, but for a special type of activity, which follows most closely the interests of the boys and girls.

"The curriculum," writes Professor Collings in a letter to us, "is a project curriculum in every respect and is organized entirely around the natural projects of boys and girls. The traditional school organization is completely ignored. The function of the curriculum, we believe, is to further the continuous growing of junior high school boys and girls *at their time,* and *in their measure.* We have excursion projects, or purposeful study of community problems, because exploration of their own and other people's environment is a normal phase of their expanding life. We have story projects, in their various forms, dramatization, story telling, reading, because at this age, it is almost impossible to supply the demand for stories. Of course play projects are a vital part of their interests. The more vigorous and challenging the play, the more it appeals to them. Football, base ball, basket ball, all forms of athletics, as well as dancing, singing, etc., are always popular. And of course young people like to make things; hence our hand projects in wood, metal, leather, repair jobs, cooking, sewing and the like. Finally we have discovered that this age enjoys mastering a technique or skill, running a typewriter well, playing a musical instrument, learning how to debate.

"No attempt is made to teach any of the traditional subjects as such. The pupils choose, plan, execute and judge their own activities under the guidance of the teachers. They budget their own

time. The daily schedule is of course extremely
flexible."

The experiment has not progressed far enough
to yield statistical results, but it is significant that
Professor Collings is not proposing to apply the
conventional standardized tests to measure the
amount of information or skill acquired. Professor Collings literally does not care whether
or not a youngster can memorize a given alge-
braic formula, or a row of historical facts.[7] What
he wants to know is how far has a school like
the present one succeeded in changing the children's conducts in their own "life acts." How
much better can they initiate, choose, understand
their purposes, how much more intense and per-
sistent is their drive, how much more skilled are

[7] To what absurd lengths teachers will go in attempting
to force their pupils to memorize totally useless material is
well illustrated in the following suggestions made in all
seriousness in a recent school publication in New York City:
MNEMONICS IN HISTORY
The present tendency in history teaching is to stress
thought and minimize memory training. But thought must
be based on facts, and memory is a storehouse of facts. It
is a problem for the history teacher to get his pupils to
memorize even a minimum number of facts. It is sometimes
amusing to a teacher to read the accounts of students who
have garbled the facts they should have memorized. Mne-
monic devices are frequently effective in memorizing essentials.
For instance, in studying the military exploits of the
Duke of Marlborough, a pupil will delight in the combination BROM, formed of the initials of the battles of Blen-
heim, Ramillet, Oudenarde, and Malplaquet. In studying
the Intercolonial Wars it is helpful to remember that the

they in initiating, choosing and evaluating the means to a given end, how much more thorough is their execution, how much better is their initiation, choice, evaluation of improvement, etc. These are the points noted in his scale, and these are measurements he is applying not only to the children in the experimental classes, but also to a group in the city schools of Norman, Oklahoma, who are pursuing the conventional high school work.

To our way of thinking, Professor Collings' experiment is a most significant contribution to education. A school which sets children free to pursue purposes that have meaning and value to them, in the pursuit of which they gain in power to initiate, to judge, to discriminate, to improve, and to press forward to ever expanding purposes,

initials of (King) William's, (Queen) Anne's and (King) George's Wars form the word WAG, and that the French and Indian War was the fourth of the series. In considering the work of the Holy Alliance it is interesting to note that Russia, Austria, and Prussia were ready to RAP all revolutionary uprising.

Another pleasant way of remembering is the use of alliteration. For instance, in the settlement of the colony of Georgia the student learns that four groups of people were the Prisoners, the Preachers, the Patriots and the Profit-Seekers.

In trying to learn the order of presidential succession this combination of the initials of the cabinet offices is helpful: ST. WAPNIACL.

This article is meant to be only suggestive of mnemoniac possibilities in history. Each teacher can devise his own combinations to aid the students in memory work.

is providing a basis for real growth, and the acquisition of the real values of life.

Below are a number of representative projects worked out by the children:

1. *Story Projects.* The children themselves dramatized the following stories:
    1. Silas Marner
    2. Courtship of Miles Standish
    3. An Indian Legend
    4. Mrs. Wiggs of the Cabbage Patch
    5. Grandmother's Wedding
    6. The Flower Fairies
    7. Hoosier Schoolmaster
    8. Pioneer Life of Grandfather
    9. Tom Sawyer
    10. Penrod
    11. Chester Gump
    12. King Lear
    13. Miss Minerva and William Green
    14. Huckleberry Finn
    15. Penrod and Sam
    16. Seventeen (Tarkington)
    17. Money, Money (Tarkington), etc.
2. *Excursion Projects.* Lectures, essays, and other accounts were given by the children following these excursions and investigations:
    1. How Iten Biscuits are made
    2. How Norman gets its water
    3. How the Daily Oklahoman is published
    4. How the Ford is assembled
    5. How Norman is governed

6. How James is tried in the Juvenile Court
7. How Norman spends its dollar
8. How Merit makes our bread
9. How Mr. Smith runs his bank
10. How Mr. James makes our flour
11. How the Wendell Company makes chocolate candy
12. How our homes are protected from fire
13. How our homes are lighted by the Oklahoma City Power Plant
14. How Mr. Leach runs his dairy
15. How the Sunshine Home cares for children
16. How the Oklahoma City Ice Plant makes our ice
17. How Mr. Thompson runs our historical museum.
18. How Mr. Lewis gins cotton
19. How the Wilson Packing Company prepares our meat, etc.

3. *Hand Projects:*
    1. How we prepared our luncheon party
    2. How Sam made his radio
    3. How John removed the water from our aquarium
    4. How Willie made his aeroplane
    5. How Mary made her cooking apron
    6. How Lillie made her house rug
    7. How Bill made his library table
    8. How Fannie made her jewel box
    9. How Sarah made her leather hand bag
    10. How Jane made her flower basket
    11. How Thomas made his hall tree
    12. How Lula made her Easter dress

13. How James repaired his phonograph
14. How Mary made her Indian blanket
15. How Margaret made her table scarf
16. How Lillie made her boudoir cap
17. How Bob upholstered his rocking chair
18. How Fannie made her Indian moccasins
19. How Jennie made her card case
20. How George made his puttees
21. How Christine made her Indian basket
22. How Jane made her serving tray
23. How William made his nut bowl
24. How Susie made her Indian vase
25. How Celia made her Egyptian bowl
26. How Reta made her Valentine cards
27. How Lorena made her painting of Snow-bound, etc.

4. *Skill Products:*
   1. Cartooning Club
   2. Sign Painting Club
   3. Poster Club
   4. Illustrator Club
   5. Sketch Club
   6. Reading Club
   7. Debating Club
   8. Public Speaking Club
   9. Good English Club
   10. Folk Dancing Club
   11. Pep Club
   12. Orchestra Club
   13. Violin Club
   14. Boys' Glee Club
   15. Girls' Glee Club
   16. Folk Song Club

17. Operetta Club
18. Costume Designing Club
19. First Aid Club
20. Camp Craft Club
21. Watch Your Step Club
22. Parliamentary Club
23. Handwriting Club
24. Spelling Club
25. Typewriting Club
26. Social Etiquette Club
27. Piano Club
28. Short Story Club
29. Puzzle Club, etc.
5. *Play Projects:*
    1. Tennis
    2. Football
    3. Basket ball
    4. Volley ball
    5. Track
    6. Baseball
    7. Boxing
    8. Tumbling
    9. Wrestling
    10. Swimming
    11. Hiking
    12. Skating
    13. Indoor baseball
    14. Balloon ball
    15. Ball Push
    16. Dodgeball
    17. Easter Party
    18. Hallowe'en Party
    19. Valentine Party, etc.

V

BEGINNING AT THE BEGINNING

To laymen, to parents particularly, the outstanding contribution of modern psychological research is the emphasis placed on the early years of childhood. These years, it is now generally agreed, are by far the most important of the entire life span, emotionally and mentally, as well as physically. Some authorities go so far as to claim that the main patterns of the future personality are already fixed by the end of the second year. "We believe," says Dr. Watson, the behavior psychologist, "that by the end of the second year the pattern of the future is already laid down. Many things which go into the making of this pattern are under the control of the parents, but they have not been made aware of them. The question as to whether the child will possess a stable or unstable personality, whether it is going to be timid and subject to rages and tantrums, whether it will exhibit tendencies of general over or under emotionalism, and the like, has already been answered by the end of the two year period." [1]

Psychoanalysis reveals many instances where severe emotional shocks experienced during the first years have produced serious maladjustments in later life. Dr. Watson in describing the method used by him in instilling the fear of a white rat in an eight-months-old baby, added that he believed it highly ‘probable that the child's fear of the animal would always persist, unless it could be overcome by some stronger counter emotion. Similar fears and emotional states are daily created in babies at the hands of well—or ill—intentioned parents or nursemaids.

These laboratory conclusions are now beginning to be reflected in the field of social endeavor. The baby is no longer regarded merely as the "young animal" portrayed in the mother's manual whose development is completely served by proper diet, proper sleep and proper airing periods. Problems of milk, teeth, rickets, adenoids, weight, contagious diseases are important, but so are questions of mental hygiene, emotional and social habits and personality traits. The habit clinic for the correction of behavior disorders is sup-

[1] "Studies in Infant Psychology," by Dr. John B. Watson and Rosalie Rayner Watson, *Scientific Monthly*, December, 1921, p. 494.

plementing the infants' milk depot, and in Massachusetts is a regular part of the State Health Department. Not only research bureaus of leading universities like Columbia, Yale and Harvard, but also leading organizations, such as the American Child Health Association, the American Association of University Women, and the American Federation of Women's Clubs are making the pre-school age a subject of special study and investigation, and nursery schools, both under their auspices and that of progressive educational institutions are multiplying rapidly.[2]

At the same time doctors and scientific men generally are reminding us that little is known of the capacities, needs and norms of children below school age. Even their physical requirements have been overlooked. As Dr. Arnold Gesell of Yale tells us, the period below school age exceeds all others in mortality and morbidity. Of all the deaths in the country, over one-third are those of children below six years. Most of the physi-

---

[2] Miss Harriet Johnson, director of the Nursery School of the New York Bureau of Educational Experiments, and one of the pioneers in the movement, has recently obtained information from some thirty-six nursery schools all over the country. Data were secured by means of a questionnaire and related to such matter as fundamental objectives, whether child welfare or research, affiliations with child welfare or educational organizations, kind of occupations and equipment, the training of teachers, and nature of research, if carried on.

cal, as well as mental defects of school children originate in the pre-school years. A table published by the New York City Bureau of Child Hygiene, based on a study of 1,061 children between four and six, and on 243,416 examinations of school children, revealed that the younger children uniformly had a larger percentage of physical defects than the older ones. These defects included hypertrophied tonsils, defective nasal breathing, malnutrition, defective teeth, pulmonary and cardiac troubles, nervous disorders, orthopedic defects. Dr. Gesell quotes figures to show that a large proportion of all cases of blindness occur in these first years, three-fourths of the deafness, one-third of the crippled and fully eighty percent of the speech defects. Practically every case of mental deficiency and an important group of mental disorders, the psycho-neuroses, as well as border-line conditions, may all go back to very early childhood. Society might be saved many incompetents by paying proper attention to the earliest abnormalities of childhood.[3]

In order that abnormalities may be easily recognized, it is necessary that we should more generally know how children normally develop. If the early years are of such fundamental im-

[3] "The Pre-School Child: from the Standpoint of Public Hygiene and Education," Houghton, Mifflin Company, 1923.

portance, it is vital for us to have precise knowledge of how children grow, and what influences
and conditions make for the best development.
Recently three studies have been published which
throw light on this relatively unexplored field.
One investigation was made by Dr. Gesell, who
for six years surveyed systematically the ordinary
and normal behavior of children from birth
through five years of age.[4] Another study was
made by Drs. Baldwin and Stecher of the Child
Welfare Research Station of the University of
Iowa, who observed and tested 105 children over
a period of from one to three years in the laboratory nursery school of the university.[5] The third
report was made by Dr. Buford Johnson, formerly psychologist of the New York Bureau of
Educational Experiments, who based the major
part of five years' study on the children in the
Nursery School of the Bureau and the City and
Country School affiliated with it.[6] The findings
of all these reports are offered tentatively and
should be so accepted, especially by lay workers.

Dr. Gesell's observations which represent a behavior study of first importance are presented not

[4] "The Mental Life of the Pre-School Child," by Arnold
Gesell, The Macmillan Company, 1924.
[5] "The Psychology of the Pre-School Child," by Bird T.
Baldwin, and Lorle I. Stecher, D. Appleton & Co., 1924.
[6] "Mental Growth of Children," by Buford J. Johnson,
E. P. Dutton & Co., 1925.

only with scientific precision, but with much human insight as well. Such homely—and thrilling —facts as when the baby first splashes in his bath, when he first holds his head erect, when he rolls over from back to stomach, when he first tries to stand, to creep, to walk, to bang with a spoon, all these overt evidences of development have been placed in their appropriate points in an ascending scale. "A man," says Dr. Gesell, "may be as old as his arteries, but an infant is as old as his behavior. In the very nature of things an infant can do neither more nor less than the maturation and organization of his behavior patterns permit. An interpretation of developmental status in relation to chronological age and personal-social environment is the diagnostic basis for safeguarding the mental welfare of the pre-school child."

Fifty normal children were tested and observed just after birth and at 4, 6, 9, 12, 18, 24, 36, 48, and 60 months of age. The results were codified into a set of schedules containing in all as many as 150 items. These items were grouped under four main headings: motor, language, personal-social (social experience and personality traits), adaptive behavior (general capacity to exploit the environment or to adjust to imposed standards). Dr. Gesell had the wisdom not to make his items into a fixed and inflexible psychometric scale. His

purpose was to devise an adjustable clinical instrument, and he has already tested it out practically in the Yale Psycho-Clinic with good results.
He is careful however to warn his readers that
this instrument will not operate automatically, objective measurements must always be supplemented by clinical judgment. "The problems of
pre-school development are still so undefined and
so complicated with possible medical factors that
considerable clinical caution must be used in applying norms and standards." "A difference of
two weeks or a month may make a great deal of
difference in the score in the first year or two,
particularly in the field of language. Delay in
walking may be due to rickets, not to subnormal
intelligence. Some children perhaps develop more
by spurts than others. There are always individual differences.'

Not the least interesting part of the study was
the comparative observations of eight pairs of
children, a four months versus a six months old
baby. a six months versus nine months, and so on
up to four years versus five years. Pedagogues
and parents may well heed the comment at the
end of these observations: "The last examination
pair were highly amenable when compared with
their early predecessors. They would do our
bidding; they would sit when we told them to

sit; they would await their turn; they would sur-
render even a coveted toy; they would remain
quiet for a time exposure while being photo-
graphed;—what would they not do for us? We
were left with a profound realization of their
teachability. This realization was disquieting; it
led us to think that we run a hygienic risk when
the schools are permitted to overexploit this very
teachability . . ." .

The aim of Drs. Baldwin and Stecher was also
to furnish tentative standards for measuring the
physical and mental development of pre-school
children. The children examined ranged in age
from two to six years, and were divided into three
groups in attendance at the laboratory school. Dr.
Baldwin's physical measurements are nationally
known, and this last report contains new and useful material on physical growth, the first collec-
tion available of consecutive physical measurements on any considerable number of pre-school
children.

Far less successful, so it seems to us, are the
results of the psychological and mental tests.
Drs. Baldwin and Stecher are apparently inspired
by the pedagogy of an older school. They are opposed to letting the child "just grow" and believe in a definite program to awaken wholesome
interests and attitudes, and to insure normal

growth. This definite program, needless to say, involves a good deal of old fashioned "training." "Music is played for appreciation and the habit is early established of listening quietly and not indulging in activities of one's own while music is going on." "It is interesting to see that children of the earlier ages have no conception of what it means to keep in line behind one another." "It is not possible to give the younger children much idea of design either by form or color" (a conclusion quite at variance with that of other close observers of children). When presented with modeling clay, the children were completely bewildered and "as with other material for constructive imagination, waited for the teachers to make something for them."

Such an attitude must necessarily affect the results of any inquiry as to how children normally develop. Children in a non free environment easily succumb into passivity, or react to tests in a negative or half hearted fashion, or else attempt to respond in the manner they think is expected of them. Moreover the Iowa laboratory was frankly an experiment station, the younger groups of children stayed in it only one and a half hours daily,—long enough to be tested, but scarcely long enough to adjust naturally and freely.

Dr. Buford Johnson in her book does two things

extremely well.   She provides important data bearing on the vital relationship between physical growth and mental development and she makes sound and careful appraisal of the value of such tests as are available for measuring early mental capacity.   Two tests, widely used throughout the country, the Binet-Simon tests (Stanford Revision) and the Pintner and Patterson scale of performance tests, she discovered to be inadequate for the extremes, the scores of young children especially being influenced by environmental training.   She also concluded that children grow at different rates, and that hereditary tendencies affect the rate of growth and therefore the stage of development at a given chronological age.

Less clinical, but none the less intensive observations of young children are also being made in a growing number of nursery schools, notably in the Nursery School maintained by the New York Bureau of Educational Experiments, in the Merrill Palmer School in Detroit, in the nursery schools directed by Miss Patty Hill of Teachers College of Columbia University, and also in the recently established Institute of Child Welfare Research of Teachers College, in the Ruggles Street Day Nursery in Boston, and in the Walden School in New York City.   So rapidly is the movement growing that already pressure is being brought to bear on the public school authorities in various cities to extend their supervision to children of nursery school age.

In England public control of nursery schools has long been an accomplished fact. The famous Fisher act of 1918 conferred on local education bodies power to establish schools for children over two and under five years of age. The movement has grown slowly, for despite the remarkable results obtained by the schools established, public appropriations for all kinds of educational purposes in England have been drastically reduced. But through the devoted efforts of Margaret Mc-Millan and others, the schools in existence are extending their influence and are an indispensable part of the public educational system. In a Board of Education memorandum, the functions of the nursery schools are stated to be, "first to provide the close personal care and medical supervision of the individual child, involving provision for its comfort, rest and suitable nourishment; and second, definite training, bodily, mental and social under the guidance and oversight of a skilled and intelligent leader, and the orderly association of children of various ages in common games and occupations. It (the school) is much more than a place for minding children . . . the influences which an adequate supply of efficiently managed nursery schools could exercise upon both parents and children can hardly be over-estimated."

It is interesting also that a distinction is made in England between nursery schools and day nurseries. The latter are controlled by the Ministry of Health, which has specifically stated that wherever possible children over three should attend nursery schools instead of day nurseries.

The whole nursery school movement in England has been largely motivated by social considerations. It has been part of a general campaign against ignorance, poverty and neglect. To quote Margaret McMillan, "In our teeming streets, and crowded warrens there live and move nearly two millions of little children who have no nursery but the streets, no playground but a dark court or a narrow and crowded room where a whole family lives and moves like birds in a cage. They suffer. They sink into ill health, into mental slackness or stupor. They fail as producers of wealth, as fathers and mothers, as citizens. And the state pays for them great sums to keep many of them in a wretched world.[7]

In America, the nursery school has been largely used as a means of scientifically studying young children, and discovering what conditions best fos-

[7] "The Nursery School in the Old Country," by Margaret McMillan, *Progressive Education*, Jan., 1925.

ter their development. Until recently, the children
attending our nursery schools have been drawn
mainly from homes of well to do and professional
people, who have been interested in the scientific
observation of children, and who have also realized that the nursery school was better organized
to meet the needs of young children than the
average home. For with the best of intentions,
what can the average parent do to provide the
necessary space, equipment and play material so
vital to the earliest years? Even in the suburbs
and small towns, practically no consideration is
given in the construction of houses to the question
of the needs of young children. Professor M. V.
O'Shea of Wisconsin recently had a survey made
of the houses of a mid-western city to find out
whether in their building any thought had been
given to the possibility of young children living
in them; he discovered of course that the possibility had not affected the house plans in any way.
The general attitude of the house owners was
one of surprise that babies or runabouts need
any special arrangements.

Yet when one considers what the natural activities are of these early years, the inadequacy of
the average home appears at once. How much
running, sliding, jumping, climbing, throwing,
pulling, swinging can a child of two or three do

in the ordinary city flat, or tidy little house in a restricted residential block? What ambitious floor schemes for building houses, or laying tracks, or constructing cities, can he carry out in a living room filled with adult furniture, how much unhindered experimenting is he permitted with hammer, nails and saw, with paints, crayons, clay, beads and weaving materials which in the course of use are likely to become "messy" in unskilled hands? How much "bossing" must he submit to on the part of older brothers and sisters? How much over-solicitous or nagging attention does he receive from his mother and other grown-ups about him? How much sheer vacuity falls to his lot—if he be city bred—aimless walking up and down a stony pavement, hand led by an indifferent nurse who airs him by the clock?

The nursery school at least attempts to provide a set-up suitable to the child's own level. It ordinarily offers ample space, both indoors and out, large play apparatus—slides, see-saw, ladders, big packing boxes, swings, sandboxes, to afford him free use of the larger muscles and chance for physical adventure—and also plenty of materials that can be put to creative use, blocks, wagons, beads, clay, paints and toys of all kinds. A healthful regimen of play and rest is observed, and in those schools which provide all-day care, question

of food and naps receive due attention. Many a
child learns to eat spinach for the first time in
the nursery school or to go to sleep promptly and
independently at nap time.

There are also certain more subtle advantages
in the nursery school over the average home which
are provided in greater or less degree. The child
without being weaned entirely from his mother
at least is freed from her sometimes too close
supervision for several hours each day. He becomes more self directing, less dependent on her
approval or disapproval, more interested in doing
things for their own sake, and not to get a response from her. The mother on the other hand,
is apt to become more objective in her attitude
towards her child when she observes him in a
group of a dozen others of the same age, and
notes how an expert, skilled in handling children
meets situations as they arise. She may learn
for the first time that coercion, sharp commands,
expectation of instantaneous obedience, or undue
emotional displays on her part are more serious in
their effect on her child than feeding him the
wrong kind of food, or permitting him to catch
cold. Many an unfortunate personality trait in
a youngster, such as excessive timidity, or pug-.
nacity, or aggressiveness or unwillingness to co-
operate, has been traced to faulty home condi-

tions and with patience and wise guidance has been made to disappear.

Moreover the nursery school provides the most natural way for young children to associate with others of their own age on equal terms. While these social contacts must often be made gradually and the child, in the beginning at least, protected from too violent or too stimulating association with his fellows, there is no question but what he gains immensely from such contacts. The assumption that children of this age are essentially individualistic is only partly true. Young children are far more social than adults have hitherto appreciated and profit greatly from group activities, and free association with one another. If not regimented or forced into conventional modes of behavior by the teacher, children can often work themselves out of undesirable social relationships into desirable ones.

To be sure a word of warning is not amiss in view of the over emphasis on socialization which one meets everywhere in current educational discussion. Because modern social life has become so complex and the interdependence of human beings so diverse, we have come to believe that we shall somehow solve the problem by plunging children into social situations at the age of eighteen months. There may be value in a highly developed social being, in a person who knows how to get on with other people, but there is also supreme value in the highly developed individual who knows how to get on with himself. The little child needs plenty of margin, plenty of leeway for the development of his personality. The jostling and hub-bub of other personalities about him have their uses, but they are not as important as is claimed by some of the zealots in the movement.

The socialization enthusiast is not the only one, of course. There is also the habit maker, the pedagogue or supervisor who has got up in advance an inventory of desirable habits, which it is believed that children should form, and sails into the nursery school room with score and note book to see whether or not they are being acquired. Many of these habits are really desirable, and children—if not coerced—will easily fall into them. Many others are entirely harmless, but others are both unchildlike and even of doubtful value. Why, for example, should a child of three or four be expected to "hold gate or door open for others," to shake hands "voluntarily with anyone," to "tell the truth" (what, may the three year old child ask, what is truth?), "wait his turn willingly," "stop crying when told to," and so on through a long list of "social-moral" habits contained in a recently concocted inventory by a graduate student of Teachers College, of Columbia University.[8]

Another danger threatening the growing number of nursery schools is that they will be staffed and supervised by pedagogues of the old school, who will merely extend to children below four years, the repressive and dreary formalism that characterizes too many kindergartens and primary grades. "Educational" activities, stressed for their own sake, or to prove some fine spun theory are likely to prevail, or else the trivial and sedentary occupations of the day nursery type.

Fortunately, modern psychological research is throwing increasing light on the kind of environment and activities necessary for sound growth. Data is accumulating to show that children in a spirited, free and enriched environment test above the average both mentally and physically. Such evidence must infallibly have its effect on nursery school development, through the nursery school on the kindergarten, and through the kindergarten, on the grades above, socializers, habit makers, and standardizers, notwithstanding.

[8] "A Tentative Inventory of the Habits of Children from Two to Four Years of Age," by Ruth Andrus, Ph.D. Published by Teachers College, Columbia University, New York City, 1924.

VI

THE USES OF MENTAL TESTING

MUCH water has run under the mill since a state superintendent of public instruction mounted the rostrum at a meeting of the National Education Association and thundered his denunciation of the proposed application of certain measuring scales to classroom work. "As well," he stormed, "as well attempt to measure the divine afflatus of a mother's love as to seek to apply scales and measuring rods to the subtle relationship between teacher and taught!"

Since then so prodigious has been the industry of scale makers and psychologists, that if the "divine afflatus" has escaped measurement, it would seem as though it were through sheer accident.[1] Scales are in the making or have been devised to measure all kinds of capacities and even such elusive qualities as will power, ingenuity, imagination, ambition and ability to appreciate poetry. One student was seriously coun-

[1] It requires some 230 pages of fine print merely to list the tests and articles about tests in bulletin, 1923, No. 55 of the U. S. Bureau of Education.

seled by the psychological department of a large
university to essay working out a scale to measure human success.   It is doubtful if any other
single subject has ever so engrossed the interest
and attention of schoolmen and psychologists as
the reputed measurement of intelligence and the
development of objective scales for gauging classroom work.   And small wonder, for if the claims
of the most ardent psychologists of this school
are to be taken seriously, the tests provide a comparatively simple instrument by which, within an
hour or two any child's mental endowment can
be ascertained, which will determine his sphere
for life.[2]   For according to these authorities, general intelligence is fixed and unchangeable, native
and inherited, and as permanent a part of a child
as blueness of eye, or roundness or squareness of
headshape.   Henceforth it will be a simple matter
to shuffle children off with a high degree of precision into various grades, each to be ticketed and

[2] Discussing backward pupils found in the upper grades,
Ruth Swan Clark of the Vocational Guidance for Juniors,
New York City, says: "As the intelligence ratings of these
pupils could have been secured in the primary grades, and
their subsequent slow progress anticipated, it is to be re-
gretted that they could not have occupied the extra two and
three years of elementary school work with training that
would have fitted them for going to work at the earliest age
when working papers are obtainable." (Some Results in
Psychological Tests in "Contributions to Education," published by N. Y. Society for the Experimental Study of
Education, 1924.)

labeled, "very superior," "superior," "average," "dull" and "very dull."   On the basis of these groupings, decision shall be made as to each child's probable future, whether he shall go to high school and college, or into the manual trades, whether he shall study for a profession or become a mechanic or manual laborer.   Certain well known private schools arbitrarily rule out children who do not come up to a certain high intelligence rating, and a recent high school department head in New York City in a published article deplored the admission into high school of any student having less than a 90 I.Q.[3]

Critics of such wholesale assertions declare in the first place that no one has succeeded in defining general intelligence, and that it is therefore absurd to pretend that the tests measure intelligence or that intelligence is something fixed by inheritance.   The attempt to group children arbitrarily is certain to work great social injustice and grave injury to those labeled as predestined inferiors or superiors.[4]   Moreover while the tests undoubtedly measure a certain kind of ability, they are largely tests of information and training.

[3] A more intelligent and sympathetic point of view is well expressed in a paper by Mabel Skinner of the Washington Irving High School, New York City, "Our Low I. Q.'s" in "Contributions to Education."

[4] See also articles by Walter Lippmann in the *New Republic,* Oct. 25, Nov. 1, 8, 15, 22, 29, 1922.

Many appeal to the type of mind that is apt at solving puzzles; in most of the tests, undue emphasis is given to ability to define abstract terms. Prepared as the tests are by pedagogues, they are based on the false assumption that success in school work is another measure of intelligence. The "intelligent" pupil is the one who is proficient in his lessons, who can easily master the ideas found in books. The one who has difficulty in understanding abstract symbols is rated "dull." Even teachers and psychologists who admit that there are important capacities that lie outside the range of the measurability of the scales, tend to patronize those who possess them. Unusual intuitive capacity, rich emotional appreciations, sensitive or artistic perceptions, are not gifts of the intellect as generally defined, and find little room for expression in the ordinary classroom, nor would they be likely to be brought to light by means of the ordinary psychological test. That little negro boy who fumbles miserably when required to reverse mentally the hands of the clock and then tell the time, has an uncanny sense of the teacher's personality; that girl who simply cannot pass the arithmetic reasoning tests, can do marvels with brush and color; that inarticulate youngster who cannot say sixty words in the required three minutes, is a new being when the

hour for music and rhythm comes.[5] Yet conceivably these children and many like them, will
as a result of "scientific" testing be graded, "dull"
or "dull normal" and be henceforth so considered
throughout life.

Yet when administered with "skepticism and
sympathy" (the phrase is Mr. Lippmann's), the
tests do have a positive value. They cannot tell
us all there is to know about a child, nor should
their findings be taken as final or irrevocable.[6]
They undoubtedly measure a certain kind of mental ability—the sort that is required to deal with
the problems of classroom work—and they may,
therefore, be a useful aid in grading children in
school. The present method of lumping all children of the same age together regardless of their

[5] "Special gifts for music and for drawing are by no
means confined to children testing high in general intelligence, but may appear in combination with I. Q. of nearly
any degree." Leta S. Hollingworth, "Experiments in the
Education of Gifted Children" in "Contributions to Education," 1924.

[6] Relative to changing I. Q. the conclusions of Dr. Buford
Johnson in her recent study of mental growth in children are
worth citing here. The I. Q.s determined by the Stanford
Revision of the Binet-Simon scale tend to increase for ages
three to six, and to decrease from seven upward, when tests
are made at intervals of a year. There is a greater inconstancy of I. Q.'s in the early years, due to marked influence
of training. Six cases of 125 changed 20 points or more;
23 changed 10 points or more. It is not probable that a
high I. Q. obtained at an early age will remain constant.
("Mental Growth of Children," p. 79, published by E. P.
Dutton and Company, 1925.)

varying capacities has proved entirely unworkable. The tests at least give official sanction to a fact never before publicly admitted by those in charge of our school systems, that children differ profoundly in mental make-up. Every classroom teacher has always been aware of this fact of individual differences. She has always realized that what she is trying to get across is over the heads of perhaps one-fourth of her class and far below the capacity of another fourth. But the course of study is constructed on the assumption that all children of a given age have approximately the same ability and that any child—unless actually mentally defective or seriously handicapped physically—can by diligent application measure up to the requirements of the grade appropriate to his age.

To be sure the educational machine erected on this assumption has long been on the point of collapse. It is now well over fifteen years since the problem of repeaters and laggards has been occupying the attention of schoolmen. Innumerable age-grade tabulations brought to light the significant fact that from one-third to one-fourth of all children in the public schools annually fail to do the work assigned to them, and must, therefore, according to the machine requirements, go through the identical process again. Busy statis-

ticians began to figure up staggering totals showing the loss to the State of this annual "repeaters" bill; others more socially minded drew attention to the iniquitous effect on the children
themselves in thus being left back and gradually
becoming schooled in failure.

How clumsily the professional educator proposes to deal with the problem, however, may be
seen from a report recently issued by the New
York Department of Education on Grading and
the Course of Study which summarizes what New
York and twenty-three other cities are doing to
lessen retardation and to modify the curriculum.
Here is a complete picture of the administrator-
pedagogue faced with a serious breakdown in his
educational machine. For that is what retardation means—millions of children annually clog-
ging the wheels of what should be a smoothly
running process. They cannot or will not follow
the prescribed course of study and when promotion time comes around and large masses
should automatically move forward, these recalci-
trants balk to the utter confusion of the operators
of the machine. What is the remedy? Abolish
the time-table, scrap the machinery, and start
afresh with the children as developing, growing,
infinitely diverse human beings? Heaven forbid!

"Our chief task," says the report, "is to speed up the 46 percent of slow progress pupils."

The "multiple track" method employed by Oakland, California, is dwelt upon at length. This provides for five general types of classes—accelerated, normal, opportunity, limited, atypical. The plan calls for a differentiated course of study, "enrichment" on one hand, and "minimum essentials" on the other. "The main consideration is to have the progress of all pupils continuous."

The curriculum and the time-table are thus the Procrustean bed in which the child, by devices nowadays scientifically determined must somehow be fitted. Never a hint anywhere in the report that fulfilling the requirements of a prescribed course of study may bear little or no relation to the learning process, that it may in fact make real learning forever impossible by destroying the child's initiative, natural curiosity and originality. Never a hint that attention to the real needs of children, to the exigencies of their growth, is the only means of insuring that what is learned has any value or gets any real hold on the child's imagination and interest. Instead, advises the educational "repair man," clip off the minutes from the time ordinarily devoted to one subject and apply them to another, "dilute" here, "enrich" there, slow up this lot, speed up this one, re-grade, re-group, measure, then compute your percentage of gains. If they are not high enough try again—on the same old lines.

The intelligence tests offer at least to bring a modicum of order out of this chaos of school grading and curriculum making. Grouping children more homogeneously as to mental capacity so that the quick and the slow need no longer interfere with one another, will set the teacher free to deal more specifically with the special requirements of her class. This should eventually lead to real differentiation in educational programs so as to conserve and develop the varying possibilities of various groups. Once rid the schoolmaster of the notion that children who are unfitted for a narrow bookish curriculum are thereby inferior to those who find book learning easy, and we may succeed in modifying the school curriculum into a truly educative instrument. That this is possible even in a large city school, where the registration ran over three thousand, is demonstrated in the unique experiment carried on for four years by Elisabeth Irwin and Louis Marks, principal, in P. S. 64, Manhattan, and described by them in their book, "Fitting the School to the Child" (The Macmillan Co.). Here we find the tests being employed for real diagnostic purposes

in order to deal intelligently with mentally defective, dull-normal, neurotic, gifted and even
a few normal children. Special classes organized
for these groups, instead of becoming mere dump-
ing grounds for various problem cases, became
genuine testing grounds for vital educational theories. Needless to say in all of them, the rigid requirements of the curriculum were relaxed and the
children were permitted a degree of freedom and
opportunity for creative expression quite unheard
of in a public school building. It should also be
noted that in addition to the tests for intelligence,
the children were given a complete physical examination, glasses were prescribed when needed, diet
corrected, so far as possible and home conditions
looked into by a visiting teacher and a health
worker.

For the most part, however, the administration
of intelligence tests is in the hands of professional
educators of the old school and they are proceeding to make them merely another accessory to the
educational machine. In New York and other
cities, the order has gone out that all children are
henceforth to be grouped in each grade according
to mental capacity, and a number of schools are
supposedly attempting to modify the curriculum
to meet the varying needs of these groups. The
testing and grading of the children according to

mental ability progress merrily enough, but the modified course of study as yet holds out little hope of genuine educational reform.

A visitor to most of these "experimental" schools would never guess that anything new or different were being tried. In each classroom are the same rigid rows held in absolute silence, the same routine, the same doling out of irrelevant and uninviting abstractions. It is, we will say, a Friday, and the weekly reviews are being given. "Take out your prefix words," drones the teacher. The class, fifty apathetic little robots, operating as a unit, slip one book off the desks and another on them. "Prefix words!" What in the name of common sense have they to do either with children or with education?

Even in the few schools where "modification" of the course of study is somewhat more advanced, the changes consist mainly in a superficial "dilution" or "enrichment," simplifying or broadening the conventional requirements. True, in the classes for mental defectives, and in the scattered groups of very gifted children, traditional methods have given way to more progressive ones, but it is significant, that for "normal" children, who are still in the majority, no changes of any sort are contemplated. For them, according to their betters, "the present course of study appears

to function most satisfactorily," the reason being no doubt that they survive it without open
rebellion. And the failure to rebel is the reason
of course why the worst abuses which afflict the
human race, continue to exist.

VII

DISCOVERING THE INDIVIDUAL

I

EARLY in the nineties, before there were any educational scales to prove it, a schoolmaster from the west dared to utter a most grievous heresy. "Children," declared P. W. Search, then superintendent of schools in Pueblo, Colorado, "children differ." They differ, he said, so profoundly and so completely that the class system so elaborately nurtured by pedagogues and administrators must be abandoned. So also must all existing types of text books, likewise most of the educational ideas held to be truest and dearest by the great majority of teachers. Each child in the Pueblo schools was thenceforth given a chance to proceed at his own rate, regardless of the progress of others.

This was the beginning of the movement for individual instruction, a movement which since it was opposed both to tradition and administrative convenience, has grown extremely slowly. Frederick Burk of the San Francisco State Normal School improved upon the Pueblo plan by a division of subject matter into units. He also, with the help of his teachers, devised a series of pamphlets suitable to individual instruction. Two of his former pupils, Sutherland and Washburne, are at present applying his methods with further modifications in the schools of Los Angeles and Winnetka, Ill. Similar experiments are also under way to a limited degree in a number of small places; in Oceano, Calif., in Racine, Wis., in Peru, Ind., Stockbridge, Mass., and Bronxville, New York.

Another associate of Dr. Burk's was Helen Parkhurst, whose plan of individual instruction, named the Dalton plan, after its first trial in the high school in Dalton, Mass., has spread across the water, and is just now taking England by storm.

In three years, the plan has been put into operation in three thousand English schools, and according to Dr. C. W. Kimmins of the University of London, formerly an inspector of the London County Council, it is destined to have a profound effect on the whole of British education. Teachers, children and parents are all enthusiastic about it. For years thoughtful teachers in England had been troubled by the insuperable difficulty of providing adequate individual instruction in their large classes. Economic necessity makes it impossible to reduce the size of teaching units, yet the results of modern psychological research and of mental testing show how greatly children differ in their ability and in their capacity to advance at a given rate of speed. In presenting a lesson to a large class, therefore, the teacher realizes that probably a bare third is following the pace she has set, that another third is capable of going faster, but is idly marking time, while the remaining children are straggling hopelessly in the rear. Under the requirements of her superiors, however, she is expected to keep this malassorted group together. By cajoling the quick, lashing the laggards, and holding the mediocre up to the mark, she must manage somehow to get the whole lot through the uniform examinations at the end of the term and into the next grade or form.

How to break up this deadening regimentation without sacrificing the important social values of the class system had appeared an insoluble problem to students of education in England, until Miss Parkhurst's plan was adopted in 1920 by Rosa Bassett of the Girls' Secondary School at Streatham. The success of the experiment was almost incredible. It excited the interest of educators throughout England, and thousands of persons visited Streatham to see the school in operation. Within a year hundreds of schools were making preparations for the adoption of the plan. It is now widely used in all sorts of English schools and colleges, primary and secondary schools, army and trade schools, manual training and normal schools. A flourishing Dalton society has been organized in London. Interest in the plan has spread to other countries, and it is being tried out in some of the schools of Russia, Germany, Austria, Scandinavia, India, China, Japan, South Africa and Australia. In America the Dalton methods are gradually winning recognition.

The Old Guard critics of everything modern in education will doubtless see in the extension of the Dalton plan merely another indication that the schools are dominated by the whims of fashion. Those who know teachers and understand their problems will not content themselves with so easy an explanation. Almost all teachers are painfully alive to their duty to instruct efficiently the children under their charge. A large proportion of them suffer chronically under a sense of failure. Teaching in such large classes as are inevitable in the modern public school produces results that no one regards as satisfactory. Education is one field in which the methods of mass production are disastrous. And the merit by which the Dalton plan has recommended itself is its bold abandonment of the methods of mass production.

Under the plan, the classroom recitation is abolished. Except for certain group activities, the children work entirely as individuals, and each child is set free to cover the required ground at whatever hours and at whatever pace seems best to him. Mimeographed sheets containing the work to be done in all subjects for a month are given each pupil and he assumes the entire responsibility for completing the assignment within the time specified if possible. As soon as he has completed one assignment he is permitted to go on with the next month's "job." He is neither hurried because some other pupils finish their assignments more quickly, nor held back because some work at a slower pace.

Fifteen minutes daily is usually set aside as "organization time," during which the pupils discuss their problems and difficulties with the class adviser. Before the close of the morning session, all the members of each grade are called into conference by the various specialists to discuss a definite part of the job and each member is called upon for his viewpoint of the work.

Instead of the classroom the Dalton school has work-shops, or as Miss Parkhurst prefers to call them, "laboratories," each fully equipped for a special subject. Maps, pictures and globes, the sand table and other necessary equipment are collected in the geography laboratory, and in an adjoining room, if possible, are placed the books, charts and apparatus commonly used for the study of history.

Each laboratory has its own teacher, a specialist whenever available, whose function is to answer questions, make suggestions and exercise a necessary oversight of the work done. It is no part of the teacher's task to hold the pupils up to the performance of a given lesson, to cram knowledge into their heads whether they will or no. The laboratories are not supervised study rooms, but rather places where the children recite, sometimes to the teacher, sometimes to one another. Primarily, says Miss Parkhurst, these laboratories are for learning. Time tables were invented for teaching, a very different matter. The Dalton plan stakes all its hopes on the wish and the will to learn of the children themselves.

This is the radical kernel in the Dalton plan. It appears almost revolutionary when one considers how educators through the ages have worked on the assumption that the child's will is an obstacle to be overcome by coercion—by threats, blows, bad marks, public disgrace—or by the cajolery of rewards or artificial interest created by applying the art of salesmanship to the teacher's wares. Only sporadically has any effort been definitely made to enlist the child's will as an active force in the learning process. Yet every one knows that outside the schoolroom the children are eager for new experiences, and go straightforwardly about the business of getting them. The initiative is there, but it can find no expression in the artificial atmosphere of the classroom with its system of bells, uniform periods and mechanical shifting from one task to another.

School living, Miss Parkhurst holds, might well take its model from home life. "At home a child moves as an individual from room to room without permission and without confusion. He goes to get something. It is this extremely simple but valuable fact that we utilize, and which makes and secures harmony and true social life under the Dalton plan." The pupils have their jobs, they know what they have to do, they go in and out of the several laboratories at will, in search of the necessary teacher or book or materials they need. Each child notes on his "job card," kept in graph form, his daily progress in terms of units of work completed. He soon learns to budget his time, and to distribute it according to his special needs and difficulties. "How a pupil manages his job or project is bound to affect his whole life.

The job tests his powers and through it, he expresses himself; he learns to evaluate himself and his work. Subject antipathies disappear; they are weaknesses which can be made to disappear by proper distribution of time." [1]

The Dalton plan is revolutionary as to method alone, not as to the content or aim of instruction. If the object of education is ability to write a letter in good English and execute arithmetical computations correctly, the Dalton method answers. It also answers if the object of education is conceived more broadly. Cultivation of individual initiative facilitates the execution of any task. This conservatism, or neutrality, in matter of content and aim seems to account in some measure at least for the widespread popularity of the plan. Old fashioned schoolmen and parents might object seriously to the substitution of newer material for the traditional subjects. They have no reason to object to a method by which the traditional subjects are learned more quickly and thoroughly.

The progressive leaders of the movement recognize that it does not in itself meet the objections to the accepted curriculum. But a curriculum, as Miss Parkhurst says, "is dead without

[1] "The Dalton Laboratory Plan," by Helen Parkhurst, *Progressive Education*, April, 1924.

the live motive power of the child." She is therefore more interested in developing that motive
power than in questions pertaining to the curriculum. The first task as she sees it is to have
"the ground made ready for the seed." This may
quiet doubts about the ultimate tendency of the
plan, but it does not wholly eradicate them. In a
Dalton school, a child may cover with the utmost
energy and eagerness all the ground required in
arithmetic, but formal arithmetical problems,
papering a mythical room for example, or com-
puting imaginary profits and losses, may be the
last thing he should be worrying his head about
at that particular time. Unless the curriculum is
carefully adjusted to the child's needs, the plan
might become the emptiest of cramming processes
with the premium put on the mere amassing of
information. It is reported that under the Dalton
plan, as one teacher puts it, "the surplus energy
of the reprobate having lost its usual means of
expression, is now absorbed in the game of passing grades." The game of passing grades is no
doubt a more useful one than many others and less
trying to the observer. But that peace for the
teacher is purchased at a heavy price if the children become so absorbed in this game as to lose
their spontaneity of preference among subjects
and activities. After all, the restiveness of the

children under the traditional method of instruction was an important force making for progress in the content as well as methods of instruction.

The Dalton plan may represent a long step in advance if it is not taken too complacently. Many schools which hesitate to initiate sweeping change may, by beginning with the Dalton plan, fall into the way of genuine educational reform. Assignments in textbooks may be supplemented by work in science laboratories, work-shops, art studios, and music rooms, as is done in the Children's University School in New York City under Miss Parkhurst's personal direction. A correlation may be made between academic and hand work, as in the Manhattan Trade School for Girls. Here the pupils in the process of learning their several trades, dressmaking, millinery, novelty making, and machine operating, have their academic work presented to them in terms of their actual work in the trade course. Arithmetic required in the cutting room is studied in the arithmetic laboratory and bears a direct relation to the work on which the girl is engaged.

II

The Winnetka plan, initiated by Carleton W. Washburne has certain points in common with

the Dalton plan.   Like Miss Parkhurst, Supt.
Washburne has abolished the ordinary recitation
and the rigid time table and put into the hands
of the children assignments prepared in advance.
There are however certain differences.

The Winnetka plan allows for more complete
individualization by subjects.   No child under the
Dalton plan may progress in any subject until
he has finished all the month's assignments in the
other subjects.   In Winnetka, there is no such
limitation.   Moreover, while the Dalton plan ac-
cepts the course of study of the school in which
it is introduced, and merely breaks it up into
monthly assignments, the Winnetka material is
prepared after long investigation of what is most
modern in type and content.   Only the three R's
or the common essentials are taught by the individual method in Winnetka.   Every child, says
Supt. Washburne, needs to know how to read
with a certain speed and comprehension, needs to
know certain elements in arithmetic, needs to be
able to spell words in common use, and to know
something about persons, places and events to
which constant reference is made.   What these
minimum essentials are in each subject, Supt.
Washburne is seeking to determine in coöperation
with other educators.   For example, the department of research in the Boston schools has

analyzed all types of addition of fractions from the standpoint of difficulties. The National Society for the Study of Education has discovered that trade and industry and the ordinary operations of life require no denominators higher than 12 in the original addends (of course the common denominator may be higher). The Winnetka teachers have carefully checked the degree of speed possible to the slowest normal child, and have found that four examples in three minutes is attainable. Therefore the assignment in addition of fractions reads thus: "Be able to work four problems in three minutes with 100 percent accuracy, the examples to contain denominators of 12 and under, to contain three addends, and to involve changing to a common denominator, addition of mixed numbers and to lowest terms." [2]

A child who is ready to begin fractions is given a fraction practice book (prepared by the teachers). This book is self-instructive. In using it, the child requires a minimum of help from teacher or classmates. Only one step is taken at a time and much practice is provided for that step before proceeding to the next. In learning to add fractions, there are some nineteen steps, beginning with the simple operation of cutting out cardboard

[2] "The Winnetka Plan of Individual Work," *The Teachers World*, Dec., 1922.

circles, cutting these in two and labeling each piece ½, and ending with a miscellaneous exercise which includes every practical difficulty in adding fractions.

Such practice books have been prepared for all elementary grades in arithmetic, for several grades in language, and also for history-geography. In time it is expected that this self-instruction material will be available in final commercial form. Already a volume has been published in spelling, and another in general science.[3]

In using these books, the child tests himself by means of an answer sheet as he completes each step, and when he has covered a given operation —such as for instance the addition of fractions— he first gives himself a practice test for it, and then goes to the teacher for a real test. This test is very complete, and is so keyed that the teacher can tell at a glance where the child's difficulty lies. No one is permitted to proceed to the next "goal" until he has successfully passed the one preceding.

The results of this method have been found by statistical study to be an increase of efficiency, a saving of one or two hours daily, and a saving of from one to three years in eight. Best of all, no child in the Winnetka schools ever repeats

[3] "The Individual Speller" and "Common Science" are both published by the World Book Company.

a grade. Thus the yearly or half yearly tragedy of non-promotion is completely eliminated.

Only half the day is given to these common essentials as the Winnetka schools are organized on the platoon plan. (See next chapter.) The other half—part of each morning and of each afternoon—is devoted to creative and group activities. Here there are no known goals, no scientific principles to act as guides. But clearly for self-expression, says Supt. Washburne, children must be given freedom and the opportunity to express what is in them. Such opportunities are provided in the multiform activities which the children undertake. There are plays, open forums, self-government meetings, debates, the publication of a school paper, to which the youngest child may contribute, and the management of which is in the hands of the seventh and eighth grade children, there are excursions, innumerable committees, free work in art, in shops and even in music. Supt. Washburne does not expect this work to be strictly correlated to the individual work. If it can, well and good. But the teachers are not required to "strain" themselves to bring into social or group activities, arithmetic, spelling, punctuation, or handwriting.

It is these special activities that seem to us the most hopeful feature of the Winnetka schools.

They are, as Supt. Washburne admits, more important than the individual work. Data may be available to prove that children save time when working individually, but time saving is not all there is to training, even in the essentials. Moreover according to recent educational thinking, it is a serious mistake to divorce the tool subjects from "life situations," and to introduce the element of drill before the pupil himself becomes aware of the necessity for it.

There are also certain unanswered questions which apply both to the Dalton and the Winnetka methods. At the 1924 Convocation of the University of the State of New York Dr. Otis W. Caldwell of the Lincoln School raised several of these questions: "Is not this plan for fragmenting and ticketing subject matter in small individual units in danger of leading us to formal and finished notions of thought units, thus producing new types of rigidity more binding than those from which we would free the pupils? Is subject matter for current social effective living capable of being set in lessons or units which can be adequately sensed without the constant suggestive thought and group experience of others of the pupils' own age and stage of life? Can the pupil be adequately educated by himself, his assignments and his skillful teacher? . . . Should not pupils gain the often disquieting knowledge that many very important considerations are still on insecure foundations and that such topics can not be presented as satisfying and finished tasks?" [4]

Neither the Dalton nor the Winnetka plans are fads, a passing fashion, to be forgotten in a brief decade. In substituting individual for mass instruction, the pupil's initiative for the teacher's coercion, they have taken a position from which they cannot be expelled. But if their results are to be really significant, they must associate themselves with reform that goes beyond method. In a really free and creative environment, children do not require the paraphernalia and rigid subdivisions of goal or contract books in order to learn the "essentials." They learn them naturally and "in their stride" as they go about affairs that have meaning and reality to them. Only under such conditions can the schools be said to minister to the individual, instead of to the standards to which they have hitherto insisted the individual must conform.

[4] *School and Society,* December 27, 1924.

VIII

WORK-STUDY-PLAY SCHOOLS [1]

It is a full decade since a series of enthusiastic books and articles were first written about the schools of Gary, Ind. John Dewey and Evelyn Dewey in their "Schools of Tomorrow," Randolph Bourne in his "Gary Schools," W. P. Burris, in his pamphlet published by the United States Bureau of Education were chief among those to draw nation-wide attention to the remarkable achievements of William Wirt and his "work-study-play" idea. Seldom has the popular notion of education undergone such rapid expansion as in the few years following these early publications. The "little Red Schoolhouse" with its humble classrooms and ill-equipped shop or two, gave way suddenly before the picture of a vast palatial structure containing art galleries and studios, music rooms and science laboratories, libraries and swimming pools, gardens and playgrounds, ten acres in size, shops of every kind,

[1] For the original source material quoted in this chapter the writer is much indebted to Alice Barrows of the U. S. Bureau of Education.

for carpentry, cabinet and paint, for foundry, forge and sheet metal work, for electricity and printing, for domestic science and sewing—all the lavish equipment of some richly endowed institution of higher learning, or a wealthy private school, now for the first time made available on so complete a scale for public school children of the elementary grades.[2] This equipment, it was explained was not extravagance, nor fads and frills. It was indeed the kind of thing long ardently desired by progressive educators everywhere, but hitherto provided only incompletely because of the prohibitive cost to the taxpayer. The Gary schools could afford them because as will be explained in more detail presently, Mr. Wirt had applied the principle of multiple use of the school plant, thus releasing funds that vould otherwise have been tied up in classroom space, for the additional facilities.

Lavish equipment however was not the only remarkable feature of the Gary schools. Says Randolph Bourne, "The Gary schools represent the fruit of a very unusual combination of educational philosophy, economic engineering, and political sagacity . . . what we have to deal with

[2] See description of the Emerson and Froebel schools in the "Gary Schools" by Randolph Bourne, Houghton Mifflin & Co., 1916, pp. 20 ff.

is an educational idea, a comprehensive plan for
the modern public school, capable of general
imitation and adaption to the needs of other
American communities." Among the many important achievements and innovations which both
he and the Deweys discuss are the social functioning of the schools in the community and of
the children in their schools, the converging of all
work and study upon school life, the wide use by
adults of the school plant, the long school day,
school week and school year, the full use made by
the school of such community resources as church,
settlements, civic and social organizations, as well
as other municipal departments, the democratic
form of student government, the wholesome in-
termingling of older and younger children in
shops and laboratories, the housing of grade and
high schools in one building, and the unique relation between the training provided in the many
school shops and the maintenance of the school
plant. For the first time, according to these early
reports, there had evolved under public school
conditions a real school community which aimed
"to put the whole child to school," and to restore
to him some of his lost heritage of wholesome
work and play.

"It is impossible," says Prof. Dewey, "to
exaggerate the amount of mental and moral train-

ing secured by our forefathers in the course of the ordinary pursuits of life. They were engaged in subduing a new country. Industry was at a premium and instead of being of a routine nature pioneer conditions required initiative, ingenuity and pluck. . . . Production had not yet been concentrated in factories in congested centers, but was distributed through villages. . . . The occupations of daily life engaged the imagination and enforced knowledge of natural materials and processes. . . . Children had the discipline that came from sharing in useful activities. . . . Under such conditions the schools could hardly have done better than devote themselves to books. . . . But conditions changed and school materials and methods did not change to keep pace. Population shifted to urban centers. Production became a mass affair carried on in big factories, instead of a household affair. . . . Industry was no longer a local or neighborhood concern. Manufacturing was split up into a very great variety of separate processes through the economies incident upon extreme division of labor. . . . The machine worker, unlike the older hand worker, is following blindly the intelligence of others instead of his own knowledge of materials, tools and processes. . . . Children have lost the moral and practical discipline that once came from sharing in the round of home duties. For a large number there is little alternative, especially in large cities, between irksome child labor and demoralizing child idleness."

This conception that the schools must overcome the demoralizing influences for children of modern city life is one of Mr. Wirt's cardinal principles. It is expressed in his first report of the Gary schools written in 1908, and in his most recent pronouncements as well. "The main business of the school," he writes in 1908, "is to utilize to the best advantage the time that the child spends in school. As a matter of fact however in most sections of the city, the greatest problem of the school is to counteract and overcome the demoralizing influences of the child's life in the streets and alleys and unfortunately in many homes, so called."

In an unpublished article, "Making the City a Fit Place for the Rearing of Children," Mr. Wirt is even more emphatic. "It is absolutely necessary for the perpetuity of our race," he states, "that the relative population of the city be reduced or that the cities be made fit places for the rearing of children. The city home is no longer able profitably to occupy all the time of the child out of school. The city school does not have sufficient time for the general education of the child.

On the other hand it is the city streets and alleys, amusement halls and gambling dens, which provide activities on the average for all the children of the cities for over five hours of the day for the 365 days of the year.

"It is this life of the child during the five hours of the day in the streets and alleys that molds his character and educates him in the wrong direction. These five hours a day on the streets must be eliminated from the life of the city child before the cities can be made fit places for the rearing of children.

"The cities must have an institution that will provide constructive activities at work and play as a substitute for the present five hours a day of destructive activities. These wholesome activities for work and play should be provided in connection with the child's study school, where he may spend the day in study, work and play. Not only will the wholesome work and play be a substitute for the demoralizing activities of the streets and alleys, but planned in connection with the study school will motivate and give new vitality to the child's study hours."

The school of course has always been subject to pressure from those both within and without the school system who seek to expand or modify the curriculum in response to changing social and

economic conditions. While its response has been
slow, it is nevertheless true that the evolution of
the school curriculum parallels closely the evolution of society. The present unwieldy and con-
glomerate assortment of "subjects" contained in
existing courses of study is at least indicative of
an attempt to train children for the highly complex—and little understood—requirements of
modern life. The curriculum indeed has changed
much more rapidly than have teaching methods
and administrative organization. The simple
reading, writing and reckoning, considered sufficient in early days, could easily enough be
taught to children seated at their desks and confined for their materials to text book and copy
paper. Yet this set up with a few variations is
supposed to suffice for the manifold demands of
the existing curriculum. In a large percent of
American cities, many buildings are without
such elementary provisions as auditoriums, playgrounds or manual training shops. Even where
these features are present, the children actually
spend very little time in them. By far the greater
amount of their time is spent in their classrooms
where the teacher at her desk is supposed to dole
out appropriate amounts of music, nature study,
hygiene, physiology, drawing, hand work, besides
the more formal work in reading, writing, arith-

metic, history, geography, spelling, civics, or such extras, as thrift, Americanization, safety first or patriotism.

Mr. Wirt boldly affirmed that a modern curriculum could not be taught under such primitive conditions. Children, he declared, cannot learn through "hypodermic injections of concentrated doses of scholastic subject matter." Two or three hours daily he argued was sufficient time for children to be confined to school desks studying the formal tool subjects. For the rest of their school day, it was far better for them to be gaining experiences at first hand in specially equipped workshops, studios, science laboratories, auditoriums, and libraries, or having the opportunity for thoroughly sound physical development in gymnasiums, swimming pools and playgrounds.

Manifestly, he argued further, a classroom could easily be alternately used by two groups of children, since neither group needs to be in it more than two or three hours. Thus by skillful programming, the capacity of a given building might be greatly increased, for two sets or "platoons" of children might be kept alternating between classrooms and the special facilities. This principle of multiple use, Mr. Wirt argues, is well enough known in the management of public utilities and other adult resources. Why should it not be applied to public schools?

"The reason why the city does not meet the needs of children as it meets the needs of adults," Mr. Wirt writes, "is because the same economic principles are not applied in the operation of child welfare agencies that are applied in the operation of adult welfare agencies.

"In the city I can have a picture to look at in my public art gallery only because a lot of other people look at this picture when I do not want to look at it. I can have a park to enjoy only because a lot of other people enjoy this park when I do not want to enjoy it. . . . I can have a street car or a taxicab to ride in when I wish to do so only because a lot of other people ride in them when I do not want to. . . .

"The whole trouble is that we try to provide a school seat in a classroom for the exclusive use of each child. Then we try to have an auditorium large enough to seat all the children, which is the same thing as providing an auditorium seat for each child's exclusive use. All children play at one time at recess which is the same thing as providing for each child a playground. The same thing is true with the manual training shops, and in a measure for all child welfare facilities. Children must all be in scnool at one time and then when dismissed from school they have the opportunity to go to the library practically all at one time. . . .

"What would we think of the management of a street car company that insisted upon everybody riding to the same point and in the same direction at one time? Under such a plan, street cars would be impossible and so would every type of public service. The management of all types of public service, *excepting schools*, attempts to balance the load on their respective facilities as much as possible. The electric lighting companies, for instance, offer reduced rates for current used in the day time in order to equalize their load. In place of using the balanced load principle, traditional school managers insist on making the load on their facilities as unbalanced as possible. That is why it has been impossible for cities to provide adequate facilities for children. Without the application of multiple use and balanced load principles the people in the cities cannot do for themselves collectively through public service agencies any more than they can do as private individuals. The city has not been able, therefore, to meet the needs of its children to the extent that it has met the needs of adults. . . ." [3]

[3] Unpublished report of the School Building Survey of Portland, Ore., conducted by U. S. Bur. of Educ., 1923.

In a work-study-play school however, the "load" is distributed between the classrooms and the various facilities. Instead of all children being in school seats when school begins, half will be in their classrooms, one-fourth in manual training, music, art, science, history and geography rooms, one-eighth will be in the auditorium, and one-eighth in the physical training and play places. In a school for 1,200 children, only 600 school seats will be needed for classrooms, 300 seats for special activities, 150 auditorium seats and play space for 150.

The money saving is obvious. A classroom costs approximately $12,000. In a 30-class Wirt school, therefore, only 15 classrooms would be needed, making available 15 times $12,000 for additional facilities. Naturally the amount saved depends upon how many additional facilities are secured. Superintendents of nineteen school systems reported to the U. S. Bureau of Education increases in housing capacity ranging from ten to seventy percent.[4] In studying the future building needs of Portland, Ore., the Survey Committee recently concluded that estimates for a satisfactory school plant on the traditional plan by 1937 showed that $23,962,150 would need to be expended, and that an excess capacity in the entire city of only 132 classes would thus be provided. On the work-study-play plan only $14,564,650 would need to be spent, providing an excess capacity of 206 classes. The difference in cost therefore is approximately $9,397,500 for the thirteen years or an average annual difference of $722,873. This amount can be saved annually to the taxpayer.

Similarly in Detroit, where the platoon school is in operation in eighty buildings, a study was made of comparative costs in fifteen schools of the platoon and non-platoon form of organization. It was found that the same number of pupils taught under the non-platoon organization could by the introduction of the platoon plan receive more instruction by the use of thirty less rooms, and 15.9 fewer teachers. The thirty rooms with a capacity of forty each, might be used to house 1,200 more pupils. . . . Even though additional salaries must be paid to auditorium and gymnasium teachers in the platoon schools, the net annual saving in salaries under this plan would be $21,820. "Thus," concludes Deputy Superintendent Spain, "good salaries can be apportioned highly trained special teachers, and the

platoon system still prove more economical than
the non-platoon." [5]

Mr. Wirt however everywhere makes clear that
"while the work-study-play plan does make possible a substantial saving to the taxpayer, that is
not the primary purpose of the work-study-play
school. It is the purpose of this school to make
the cities good places in which to rear children.
No other question is of more vital importance to
the American nation."

This feature of "multiple use" has commended
the Wirt type of school organization widely to
practical schoolmen throughout the country.
Although the attempt to introduce the plan into
New York City failed disastrously in 1917, due
mainly to political opposition, it has been spreading with increasing momentum in other parts of
the country. The name now generally adopted is
the "platoon" school, although "work-study-
play" and "duplicate" schools are terms also
widely in use. The latest list of cities having
such an organization in one or more schools
numbers ninety-three in thirty states, and includes such large centers as Pittsburgh and Detroit, which have officially adopted it for all
elementary schools, and also Philadelphia, Balti-

[5] "The Platoon School," by Charles L. Spain, Ph.D., New
York, The Macmillan Company, 1924.

more, Newark, Rochester, Cleveland, St. Paul, Dallas, Sacramento, Seattle and Portland, Oregon. So interested have superintendents of schools become in the plan, that the United States Bureau of Education has called four annual conferences on it to discuss practical problems of administration. The conferences are held in conjunction with the meeting of the Department of Superintendence of the National Education Association. Eight national committees appointed by the Commissioner of Education, are constantly at work, gathering material to report to the conferences on such questions as use of the auditorium, building program, organization, training of teachers, music, special activities, play and education of public opinion. Several teacher training schools and summer schools have included special courses on some aspect of the plan.

The plan has been adapted in many different forms. No two programs are the same, the length of the school day varies from city to city, so also does the kind and amount of additional equipment and facilities provided, the amount of departmentalizing of subject matter, the use made of the auditorium, and the amount of vocational training afforded. No city has adopted all the interesting features of the Gary schools. Gary is still unique in the broad use by adults of the school plant, in the eight hours school day, in the large voluntary attendance of children and adults in Saturday and summer school, in the degree to which vocational work contributes to the maintenance of the school plant, and many other innovations. It is of course also true that some cities have adopted the platoon organization merely or mainly as an economy device, or to relieve congestion, and have added few additional facilities to existing plants.

By far the greater number of superintendents experimenting with the plan, however, have been impressed by its educational possibilities. In discussing its possibilities, these men use language quite different from the old type "administrator." Says W. F. Kennedy, director of Platoon Schools in Pittsburgh:

The following are the objectives that largely determined the activities and organization in the early days of our experiment (1916) and still control the movement:
  I. Enrich children's experiences.
      a. An enriched curriculum.
      b. Enriched teaching.
      c. Enriched associations.
      d. Fresher interests native to child life.
  II. Socialize and democratize the activities of school life.
  III. Develop an atmosphere in terms of departments, an attitude of hunger for worthwhile

pursuits and habit of planning in children, and a growing vision of something ahead.

IV. Emphasize the *process* in education rather than the product.

V. All educational development should be based on the native characteristics of children, such as activity, curiosity, imitation, imagination, desire to work with tools and materials, etc.

VI. School life should be made pleasant. Happiness is an important educational objective.

The above objectives controlled the selection of teachers, the organization of the curriculum, and the working out of the whole schedule of operations. It meant that teachers should teach those subjects with which they were in tune, for which they had an appreciation and definite preparation. It meant that the characteristics of childhood and the demands of life should be largely the basis of the selection of the subjects of the curriculum. It meant that opportunity should be furnished to pupils to express themselves naturally, to practice self-control, to exercise initiative and responsibility, to appreciate freedom, and to develop poise and personality. It meant that teachers were to be helpers, leaders and friends of children, and not checkers, detectives and faultfinders. It meant that children should have a voice in working out plans, suggesting situations and criticizing results. And it definitely meant that this school should have the atmosphere of a cheerful home, and if joy and happiness were not constantly in evidence some part of the machinery was wrong.

A number of superintendents who have experimented with the plan, discuss its advantages in terms of the educational philosophy of John Dewey and William Kilpatrick. "The platoon school," writes C. F. Perrott of Stuttgart, Arkansas, "is a distinct and important factor in the educative process. . . . It creates an opportunity for an enriched curriculum for all our school children, more especially of the elementary schools. . . . It is a known fact that only one-fifth of our elementary school pupils ever reach high school. . . . The dull routine of our elementary school is largely responsible.

"In the platoon school, the shop, laboratory, garden, libraries, dramatization, play and games are used freely. Dewey says of this that where such opportunities exist for reproducing life situations or progressive experiences, we have real thinking. Such thinking is possible where besides the ordinary classrooms we have playgrounds, shops, music and drawing studios, gymnasiums and intimate and constant contact with supplementary activity outside the school for the children. . . . When thought is continually hedged in by authority, courses of study, the four walls of a classroom, and continual silence, thinking instead of being encouraged is thwarted at every point. . . .

"The development of the platoon school is undoubtedly in great part an outgrowth of the idea that extrinsic subject matter does not permit the fullest life. Dr. Kilpatrick is of the opinion that since the elementary school is an institution established by society for the education of its children, it would seem that its most consistent function would be to provide an environment that furthers the continuous growing of its pupils, an environment that affords them practice in the selection and successful realization of aims. I am not going to insist that the platoon school is ideally fitted and suited to carry out this philosophy. At the present time it affords the nearest approach to a solution of the problem that we have. . . ."

Other advantages observed by superintendents after a trial of the plan include improved health of pupils, increased self-control, initiative and independence, happier attitude towards school— "the children are decidedly for it"—fewer disciplinary troubles, less fatigue and monotony, it minimizes lockstep, socializes the school, subject matter better handled by teachers, who have fewer subjects to teach, and certain subjects are taught by those specially fitted for them, . . . "it does away with listless teaching through an enriched curriculum which makes the teacher aware of the breadth of the child's needs, mentally, physically and morally. . . . It places a better proportion and value upon both mental work and all other activities. . . ."

One result worth perhaps special emphasis is the improvement recorded in academic work. This is encouraging because the unfavorable showing made by the children in Gary schools at the time of the survey of the General Education Board, received wide publicity. In 1922, another survey was made in Indiana. Tests were given in reading, spelling, arithmetic and history to children in Gary and in other school systems in the state. Returns showed that the Gary children scored higher in all grades in history and geography than children in other Indiana cities. In particular, the scores of Gary children in thought questions in history were five to seven points higher than those of children in traditional schools. In reading and spelling, Gary children did better in three grades and not so well in others.[6]

In 1923, the Department of Educational Research of Detroit made public the results of a study carried on for several years of the academic standing of children in platoon and non-platoon schools. Standard tests were applied in reading, penmanship, arithmetic, spelling, and geography.

[6] Data secured from U. S. Bureau of Education.

"Taken as a whole," writes Stuart A. Courtis, Director of the Department of Instruction, Teacher Training and Research, "the results from standard tests show that in both actual and comparative achievement, in efficiency of instruction, in type of school affected, and in the efficiency of supervisory control, the platoon schools in Detroit have, so far, done fully as well as, and probably better than the conventional schools as far as instruction in the drill subjects is concerned." [7]

Tabulations, based upon a study of results over a period of four years, showed that the schools organized four years ago were far above the city median; those organized three years ago were also considerably above; and those organized less than two years, who were passing through a period of readjustment were slightly below the city median, but constantly improving their scores.

An item from the Clip Sheet sent out by the United States Bureau of Education for June, 1925, states that of fifth grade children in work-study-play schools in Gary, seventy-five percent reach the eighth grade. Fifty-three percent of all high school graduates from the same schools go to college. Twenty percent of all children who enter elementary schools in Gary enter college in

[7] "The Platoon School in Detroit," by Charles L. Spain, The Detroit Educational Bulletin, No. 2, 1923, p. 66.

due course: that is three times as many as the corresponding ratio for the country at large.

The platoon school has been attacked by both
conservatives and radicals in education. It has
also unfortunately been opposed by powerful political groups. The argument used with such
deadly effect during the Mayoralty campaign in
New York City, that the Gary plan is a device
of the "interests" to fit the child for the mill and
sweat shop, is of course not worth serious attention. At least it would not be had not a rather
considerable number of otherwise intelligent
labor [8] and socialist organizations also given it
credence. The argument first had its basis in the
large amount of training offered to children in
Gary schools to "work with their hands," in
specially equipped shops of all kinds. When the
educational value of such activity was made clear,
the argument shifted its base. Recently it has
taken refuge in the departmental system of teaching which obtains in greater or less degree in all
platoon schools.

In her minority report of one on the work-
study-play or platoon plan, submitted to the Chicago Board of Education by the Education Com-
mission appointed by the Board in December,

[8] In June, 1924, the Detroit Federation issued a favorable
report on the Detroit platoon schools.

1923, Rose A. Pesta writes of the departmental system: "It is exactly the factory system applied to the education of the child. In the olden days a pair of shoes was made by one man. He put something of himself into the shoe—his individual art—and he took a certain pride and joy in the completed product. In modern industry, the shoe passes through a number of hands, each doing a little here, a little there. Each is interested in doing efficiently his little job—not in the completed job at all. That is what is recommended in the education of children in so far as they receive an education in special lines; each of the special teachers doing her little bit toward the education of that child with no possibility of any interest in the complete process. . . ."

The controversy over departmental work is of course an old one, and has long been waged outside the realm of the platoon school. Teachers of special subjects have for many years been appointed in the upper grades of most school systems. In most private schools, where groups are of course smaller, it has been carried far down into the primary classes. Those in favor of it claim that teachers teach subjects best in which they are most interested, that it is unreasonable to expect one teacher to teach successfully the ever-increasing subjects in the modern curriculum, that

it is better for children to come into contact with
different personalities, and with different methods
of presentation.   Opponents claim that children,
young ones especially, need the "mothering" influence of a single individual, that specialist teachers tend to exploit their specialty at the expense
of those they teach, that under them a child's day
loses unity, that successful "project" teaching,
now everywhere urged, is incompatible with de-
partmentalization, that special teachers cannot
possibly keep in personal touch with their pupils
since they meet several hundred a day, and many
more during the week, that the whole trend of
educational thinking is away from a curriculum
organized on a subject basis, to one organized on
a conduct or activity basis.[9]

A partial answer made by those in charge of
work-study-play schools is that only part of the
work is departmentalized.   At least two and a
half hours daily is spent by each child in its
"home" room, under one teacher who teaches all
the tool subjects.   This arrangement is in turn
criticized by those who feel that it is a mistake to
divorce the tool subjects from the subjects in
which the tools are used.   A child should not be

[9] See "Why I am Opposed to the Platoon Plan in Elementary Schools," by Frederick G. Bonser of Teachers College, *Chicago Schools Journal*, May, 1924.

drilled in arithmetic in vacuo, but only when he is aware of a given situation where drill is necessary.

"Arithmetic," writes Dr. Kilpatrick, "we shall always need and shall always teach. The point is this. We learn better—certainly as a rule—when we face a situation calling for the use of the thing to be learned. Other things being equal then, we shall try to teach arithmetic as it is needed. that is in connection with situations of actual need. The effect of this will be to find arithmetic in many little pieces scattered along the path of life. These we shall teach as we meet them. As we accumulate in this way a store of arithmetic, some of the pupils, particularly the more mathematically inclined, will from time to time put the pieces together and form wholes more or less complete. Later some will specialize in the subject. . . ." In the paragraph preceding this, Dr. Kilpatrick declares that "separate subjects for children will have to go." [10]

This is of course going very much further than the work-study-play idea now proposes. The platoon school has accepted the modern curriculum with its many subject divisions, and has attempted to give it reality and vitality through ad-

[10] "Foundations of Method," by William H. Kilpatrick of Teachers College, The Macmillan Company, 1925, p. 357.

quate equipment and a well balanced program of activities. The plan makes no changes in classroom teaching, which must inevitably change radically if real educational values are to be attained. "The present academic subjects are taught and must be, with our present limitations, taught as such," writes John G. Rossman, Assistant Superintendent of Schools in Gary. "The greater part of the work of the teacher in the platoon school is not such as to require training different from that given in the usual normal school," declares Charles A. Rice, Assistant Superintendent in Portland, Oregon. "A good teacher in a traditional school will be a good teacher in the home room in a platoon school." Similarly Edwin Y. Montanye, principal of a "duplicate" school in Philadelphia states that there is "little difficulty in securing teachers for the academic subjects."

It is probably too much to expect, however, that the work-study-play school should be more than a liberating experiment in education. Although vastly freer than the traditional school, it has not yet emerged from its stage of mechanization. To accommodate rotating groups of children smoothly and efficiently, programs must be observed with scrupulous exactness, so many minutes must be allotted to each activity, and shifts must take place with speed and promptness. The plan still tolerates class units as large as forty, and it faces with equanimity school plants housing two thousand children and more.

In brief, the work-study-play plan is a magnificent attempt at mass education, attempting, through the application of a principle well known in mass production—the balanced load—to provide wholesale advantages to children without increasing school costs. Yet when one considers the nature and variety of genuinely educative enterprises that Mr. Wirt has managed to introduce into his schools, the extraordinary value of his wholesale demonstration becomes apparent. Probably nothing has done more to free the public mind from the notion that children can be educated by being chained to school seats than the campaigns successively waged in different cities to introduce work-study-play schools. While the claim often made is valid that all the advantages of these schools exist (in part) and can be obtained in traditionally organized systems, it still remains true that the platoon organization makes it possible for communities to provide such advantages for their children years earlier than they could otherwise be persuaded to do so.

It is probable that many of the shortcomings of the plan will pass with time. Superintendents adopting it are likely to be of the temper of Mr.

Wirt who welcomes educational experimentation of every kind, even with curriculum and subject matter. "Organic education" classes directed by Mrs. Marietta Johnson of Fairhope, Alabama, were planned for certain Wirt schools in New York City. Attempts are likely to increase to introduce genuine "projects," as the common product of many departments in platoon schools. The revolt against "subject matter" as such, may finally break up much of the present undesirable subdividing of the curriculum. As for the niggardliness of a public that compels the platoonizing of a school, takes pride in school plants of enormous size, and tolerates class units of forty and forty-five children, that even too may change. One reason why, no doubt, that we as taxpayers are so loath to pay taxes large enough to eliminate such evils, is because our own memories of school are so dreary and our distrust of schooling so profound. Graduates of schools where as children they were happy, where they had the opportunity to develop naturally and fully, may be expected to have quite another attitude towards education. They may come to class education among the first essentials of life and pay for it accordingly.

IX

THREE DEMONSTRATION SCHOOLS

EDUCATIONAL reformers are of three kinds:
those who accept the established body of knowledge as necessary for the child to learn, but who
admit that the methods of presenting it are at
fault and must be changed; those who advocate
changes in the curriculum so as to prepare children more adequately for a modern world; and
those who view education as an organic process
which changes and develops as the child himself
changes and grows. None of these three groups
works entirely independently. The difference in
emphasis, however, profoundly affects what each
is doing, and the future education will be largely
shaped by the degree to which one group or the
other succeeds in dominating educational thought
and policy.

Just now the technicians are very much in
vogue; the measurement of intelligence, of classroom achievement, and improvement in method
occupying the major efforts of schools of education and professional schoolmen everywhere. The

second group is also much in evidence, demanding modern schools to fit children to play a worthy part in a modern world. The third group is only beginning to attract attention outside of advanced circles, and is still dismissed by the majority of educators as visionary.

There are in New York City three schools which, although private, are known as pace setters for the country in the first two types of reform. All three also have experimented in their lower grades with the principles held by the third group. The institutions are the Horace Mann and Lincoln schools, both officially connected with Teachers College, and the Ethical Culture School. Both the Horace Mann and Ethical Culture schools are frankly conservative as regards curriculum, save for the work of Miss Patty Hill in the kindergarten and first grade of Horace Mann and the primary grades in the Ethical Culture School. The Lincoln School, on the other hand, is frankly experimenting with the curriculum, seeking to adapt it to the changed demands of modern society.

The Ethical Culture School, established in 1878, is the oldest of the three. It was founded by Dr. Felix Adler as a free kindergarten for the children of working people, but it grew rapidly into a full graded school to which children

were admitted from all social strata. Children
are not excluded because of race, religion, or
color—a rare policy in a private school—and
scholarships, affording either full or partial tui-
tion extended to over two-fifths of the enrollment,
cut down economic barriers. In admitting children, however, preference is usually given to
those with a high record of scholarship and a
high intelligence rating—at least 115—and once
admitted, pupils are expected to meet the exacting
requirements of the school's course of study. The
result of this policy is that the school serves primarily a rather narrowly specialized intellectual
type, and necessarily excludes many children
whose special talents lie outside the range of
measurability of the scales, or who lack ability
to perform difficult academic work.

Some of these pupils are permitted to remain
and take a modified course leading to a certificate
instead of a diploma, but they are regarded rather
as lost souls by the administration. In discussing
them recently Superintendent Lewis said:

For them the thought of the world bearing on
human progress so far as it is bound up in ethics,
literature, history, science, and foreign languages
is very largely a sealed book. Facts they can
often grasp and reproduce, but the relations of
facts and reasoning generally in the abstract data

of language are often beyond their capacity. Hence they do not seem to me to be those best qualified by nature to attain the school's highest aims. . . . They are not those whose intelligence can be raised to a point where they can cope successfully with the burning problems now facing mankind.

The avowed purpose of the school is to train ethical leaders, "reformers" of society, and its officers are proud of the fact that a larger proportion of its graduates than of any other school are engaged in teaching, research, or some type of social service. The ideal of service to society is held constantly before the pupils by means of formal ethics instruction as well as by numerous activities on behalf of the community.

A prevocational arts course has been established in the last two years of high school for those children who show special artistic ability. It is the ultimate hope of the school to offer similar courses to those specially endowed in music, in home-making, mechanical ingenuity, and science. Even here, however, the emphasis is placed upon academic standing and intellectual capacity, for Superintendent Lewis does not believe the course will be successful with students who do not possess at least average general intelligence in addition to special talent, nor would he give preference to the dull but talented student over the bright and equally talented one.

While all the children of the middle and upper school are thus held to the requirements of a conventional curriculum, the attempt is made through psychological study of each child to provide a rounded range of activities, mental, physical, and social. This is important, for precociously intellectual children are frequently emotionally infantile, or unable to respond normally to social situations.

Some years ago an experiment was made in the primary grades of the Ethical Culture School by Miss Mabel Goodlander to test out some of the more progressive theories of education.[1] No changes were made in size of class or in room space, but complete freedom was given in the selection of materials, use of class time, and employment of special teachers. Miss Goodlander's aim was "to create a free social environment where children in coöperation with others of the same age might make a beginning in democratic living under conditions more like life outside school than commonly considered appropriate for the school régime." Children as well as teacher

[1] See "Education Through Experience." By Mabel R. Goodlander. Bulletin No. 10, New York Bureau of Educational Experiments.

were at liberty to sit where convenient, talk and move about freely so long as they did not annoy others, and to work or play either as individuals or in groups. Although the teacher directed the class when necessary, the children were mainly engaged in projects of their own.

It is one of Miss Goodlander's cardinal beliefs that the teacher must never dominate the situation. "We must learn," she says, "to appreciate more sympathetically each child's point of view, and we should be willing to accept his judgment in many things frankly and sincerely even when it differs from our own."

As regards curriculum the emphasis was shifted from formal studies to constructive work and play, to expression in varying art forms, and to first-hand knowledge of social and industrial activities related to the child's life. The three R's were mastered, but Miss Goodlander waited until the interest of the children in them had been naturally aroused.

Miss Goodlander carried her experiment forward with the same group for four years, and then started with a new class. According to Superintendent Lewis the experiment was a success, tests showing that as compared with two parallel divisions Miss Goodlander's group met the school's requirement in formal work and excelled in ability to observe, initiate, and carry projects through; in coöperation it was superior to one group and inferior to another.

In the fall of 1924 a branch of the Ethical Culture School was opened in the West Seventies under the direction of Miss Goodlander, who can now more thoroughly test out and develop her earlier experiment. The classes are housed in a large old fashioned dwelling which admits of a sense of intimacy and naturalness so important for young children especially. The grades are limited to the first four, and the kindergarten and the class registers are kept down to fifteen. The groups are therefore small enough for the development of individual ability, but large enough to encourage social and coöperative activities. The program is extremely flexible, the children are allowed much freedom in choosing and directing their own work, in shop, play and the arts, no less than in the more formal subjects. The classes stay all day, and have plenty of time outdoors both in the park nearby, and visiting places of interest in the city. Even all day Saturday trips to the country are planned. The children are fitted to take their places in the succeeding grades of the parent school, which it is to be hoped will gradually become more freed from traditional practices and outlook.

In the Horace Mann School, also, due to Miss Patty Hill and her associates, the work of the kindergarten and primary grades is less formal and more flexible than that of succeeding years. Miss Hill's work has profoundly affected the course of kindergarten and primary education throughout the country in the direction of a freer and more democratic type of organization.

Recently she has been attempting to apply the principles of behaviorist psychology to curriculum making and has worked out with her associates a series of activities designed to develop proper habits, physical, mental, emotional, and social.[2] With the help of several hundred leaders in kindergarten and primary education a "habit inventory" was first produced listing specific habits which the majority agreed young children should form. As this inventory was used, Miss Hill discovered that the supervisors and classroom teachers "began to think of all instruction in terms of desirable change in thought, feeling, and conduct." The principles of habit formation were thus gradually applied to all school subjects. "The proper conduct of the three R's became as evident

[2] "A Conduct Curriculum for the Kindergarten and First Grade." By Agnes Burke, Edith U. Conard, Alice Dalgliesh, Edna V. Hughes, Mary E. Rankin, Alice G. Thorn, Charlotte G. Garrison, Teachers of Horace Mann School. Introduction by Patty Smith Hill. Charles Scribner's Sons. 1924.

as the so-called moral and social conduct." This
resulted in regarding each aspect of the curriculum, not as a formal school subject, but as a social situation rich in activities and experiences.
Thus acquired, the habit takes on meaning and is
associated in the mind of the child with a sense
of satisfaction or pleasure.

The basis for what Miss Hill calls her conduct
curriculum is indubitably sound, and most of the
activities listed in her book are wholesome and
properly selected. There is always the danger,
however, as Miss Hill herself recognizes, that the
very explicit aims set down by her group will be
used not as means of wider freedom but of more
repression. Unhappily the moralists and discipli-
narians manage to function, no matter what instrument is put into their hands. Their natural
tendencies are not likely to be checked by the following list of "desirable" changes in thought, feeling, and conduct which should be developed:
"Learning to enter room politely," "Greeting
teachers and children courteously," "Gaining an
attitude of respect and obedience toward parents
and other adults," "Learning to use time wisely,
i.e., balance between quiet and active work" (what
young child consciously strikes such a balance?).
In "coming to group for discussion and music,"
the desirable change stressed is "learning to se-

lect right-sized chair and to carry chair properly."

These imposed standards of conduct explain much of what one observes upon visiting the primary classes of the Horace Mann School. Washing the hands before the mid-day luncheon became in one room an event of awful import, where silence was enjoined and order kept absolute. Later, the rest period, where the children were expected to relax, became a quarter hour of exasperated nagging by the teacher to enforce immobility upon thirty wriggling youngsters.

The upper grades of the school make no pretense of free activity. The standards upheld are those which have the weight and sanctity of tradition behind them, but individual teachers are allowed a high degree of personal initiative, and a variety of experiments have been carried on, especially in method, which are of distinct value. Scientific pedagogy has an important place in education, and schools everywhere are indebted to the researches made by Teachers College and applied in the Horace Mann School. It would be stimulating to those interested in adapting education to the needs of growth if the teachings of Dewey and Kilpatrick were applied more generally to the curriculum itself.

The aim of the Lincoln School, as described by its director, Dr. Otis W. Caldwell, is "to construct a fundamental curriculum which will be representative of the important activities, interests, and possibilities of modern life." In remaking a curriculum, reliance must be placed not upon the judgment of textbook writers and individual teachers, but rather upon objective studies of human needs. The school has been in existence only eight years, but has already effected a number of thoroughgoing changes in the course of study. These results have been made available to teachers throughout the country.

Chief among them is the revision of subject matter in the social studies, in junior high school mathematics and in science for the upper elementary grades. In all these subjects, new texts have been prepared which are a vast improvement over anything hitherto existing in these fields. Of special interest is the work of Dr. Harold Rugg, who has abolished the artificial divisions existing between history, geography, civics, economics, and sociology, and grouped the material under one natural heading—social studies—designed to help the student to understand and deal intelligently with the problems of contemporary life.

Dr. Rugg's approach to his job is that of the scientist. His twelve social science pamphlets, which embody for the junior high school the material as worked out to date, have been assembled after years of painstaking analysis, inventory making, trial use, and revision. The Lincoln School has obtained the coöperation of over one hundred schools scattered throughout the country which make use of the new curricular material and test out its results as compared with those of classes following the ordinary courses. Besides breaking down unnatural subdivisions between allied fields of knowledge, Dr. Rugg has substituted human episodes for the encyclopedic rehearsal of bare facts. The course is thus not only enormously enriched and vitalized, but children are stimulated to weigh and discuss the value of one episode as compared with another, to draw their own conclusions, and test the validity of data. Dr. Rugg holds that it is only through such practice that the future citizen will resort to intelligence instead of prejudice as a guide to conduct.

Besides the junior high school pamphlets, Dr. Rugg's department has made a number of other studies. One deals with the crucial problems and conditions of contemporary life, as a basis for determining what people ought to know about the industrial, political and cultural world and what tendencies to action the school should set up. Another study has been made of "frontier thinkers," those whose insight and judgments most profoundly interpret contemporary life and conduct. An investigation is also under way to determine what historical movements, epochs, events, conditions and persons are of greatest importance for adequate understanding of present day conditions and problems.

Curricular reform of this kind, Dr. Rugg holds, is basic to social progress. With Wells he believes that the current order is witnessing "a race between education and catastrophe." [3] Unless the schools can produce a generation of informed, thinking, socially disposed citizens, catastrophe is likely to overtake us. A dynamic curriculum in our schools is imperative. What such a curriculum would be like has been described for us by Dr. Rugg in a recent monograph. It would be, he says, "a curriculum which deals in a rich vivid manner with the modes of living of people all over the earth; which is full of throbbing anecdotes of human life. A curriculum which will set forth the crucial facts about the local community in which the pupils live; one which will interpret for them the chief features of the basic resources and industries upon which their lives depend in a

[3] "Objective Studies in Map Location," by Harold Rugg and John Hockett, published by The Lincoln School of Teachers College, 1925.

fragile, interdependent world; one which will introduce them to modes of living of other peoples, —the English, the French, the German for example, as typical of the industrialism of the western world, the Russians, Chinese, and the peoples of South America—types of those who live under an agricultural economy, but whose modes of living in succeeding generations will become more and more like those of the industrial world. A curriculum which will enable pupils to visualize the problems set up by human migration, one which will provide them with an opportunity to study and think critically about the form of democratic government under which they are living and to compare it with the forms of government of other peoples. A curriculum which will not only inform, but will constantly have as its ideal the development of an attitude of sympathetic tolerance and of critical open-mindedness. A curriculum which is built around a core of pupils' activities—studies of their home community, special reading and original investigation, a constantly growing stream of opportunities for participation in open-forum discussion, debate, and exchange of ideas. A curriculum consisting of a carefully graded organization of problems and exercises, one which recognizes the need for providing definite and systematic practice upon socially valuable skills.   A curriculum which deals courageously and intelligently with the issues of modern life and which utilizes in their study the cultural and industrial as well as the political history of their development.   A curriculum which is constructed on a problem-solving organization, providing continuous practice in choosing between alternatives, in making decisions, in drawing generalizations. Finally a curriculum which so makes use of dynamic episodical materials illustrating great fundamental humanitarian themes that by constant contact with it children will grow in wise insights and attitudes and, constructively but critically, will be influenced to put their ideas sanely into action.

"Such a proposed curriculum will sound visionary to many workers in our schools.   Nevertheless, ten years of close contact with curriculum-construction convince one that the characteristics described can be produced.   Their attainment will require the deepest vision and the clearest thinking our American educational scheme can bring forth.   Hard intellectual work will be demanded of many persons.   Most important of all, at the present juncture, will be the necessity of a more truly experimental attitude than is now common among those who control curriculum making."

More than a score of other curricular investi-

gations are in progress in the Lincoln School.
Notable work has already been done in revising
content and method in teaching reading, spelling,
English composition, high school literature, history, modern languages, industrial arts, music,—
in fact in practically every subject in every grade,
some degree of experimentation is going on.

Four guiding principles have been defined by
Dr. Caldwell as fundamental to the reorganization of any school subject: Subject matter and
method must be engaging and genuine; pupils
must succeed if they are to become educated; sense
training is necessary (at present education is
based too much on words and too little on touch,
sight, and taste); children should be encouraged
to work together and teach one another.

These principles find expression in a variety of
ways in the school. The curriculum of the elementary school has not been subjected to the same
analysis and study as that of the upper grades,
but the class teachers are afforded much freedom
for experimentation. The primary rooms usually
present a pleasant hubbub of activity. They are
large, sunny, and equipped with all manner of
materials—a work bench, lumber and tools, a sand
pile, large blocks, clay, paints, and large cardboard for stage scenery, with a white rabbit or
two rambling about at will. A play is frequently

in preparation and the children are busy composing it, painting the scenery, constructing buildings and furniture, and issuing invitations to parents and friends. One first grade recently dramatized the marketing of milk, while the second grade gave a play about New York, with skyscrapers, bridges, and elevated tracks complete. This play grew out of many months of work with a city made out of boxes, which was one of the important centers of interest of the grade, and around which much valuable subject matter was built. The work continued all through the year, and supplied opportunities and meaning for much of the arithmetic, English and reading. For example, rulers were used to find the lengths, widths, centers and heights of things. A great deal of work in proportions was necessary to judge the proper size of trains, furniture, cars, and trolleys to be right for the dolls who used them. Questions like the following constantly arose: "How much cloth is needed for the grocery store awning?" "How can we space the posts evenly for the railway fence; how get the posts all the same size?" Scientific problems also were discussed, "What are the reasons and methods for preserving foods in cities?" "How does it happen we have so much pure water?" "How are streets kept clean?" Excursions were taken to many parts of the city to gain needed information, to the post office, to wholesale markets, to railroad stations, and warehouses.[4]

Field work is an essential part of the activities of each grade. Last year over a hundred excursions were taken to museums, parks, factories, bridges, bakeries, markets, railway terminals, municipal and office buildings, pasteurization plants, hospitals, newspaper plants, various exhibits, etc., etc. In the earliest grades, the children frequently record their impressions of their trips in story or diary form. These records are mimeographed and bound in loose-leaf booklets, and later used as class reading material. Other activities following a trip may be: painting pictures, designs on paper or in wood or clay, map making, cooking, sewing, library reference work, collections of pictures, block play, exhibit for other pupils. The second grade children visited a vegetable farm on Long Island to discover the source of city supplies. The fourth grade went to a saw mill to supplement their study of lumber. Some of the older girls visited a mother and baby in their apartment to study the science of baby care at first hand. A seventh grade made

[4] "Making a Play City," by Katherine L. Keelor, "Progressive Education," June, July, August, 1924.

surveys of housing and street conditions in various sections of the city.

Another valuable means for supplementing and making real class activities, and of presenting material in vivid form is supplied through the school assemblies, at which a variety of programs is given by the children relating to their own special interests. So popular have the assemblies become that a weekly period has been set aside for them. Four general types have been developed: class studies assemblies, coöperative assemblies by several grades, current interest assemblies, and programs by outside artists and specialists. A ninth grade gave an assembly to tell the high school what they were doing in each subject, the high school seniors gave a poetry reading, greatly enjoyed by the elementary grades, the first grade gave a program of Christina Rossetti poems, the fourth grade gave a geography assembly. A number of grades combined to give pottery and fine arts assemblies.

These assembly periods are very different from the kind usually conducted in the ordinary schools, where the children recite set pieces, or render songs or instrumental music, made wooden and lifeless by drill. Every program in the Lincoln School assembly bears vital relation to what the children themselves are doing. The children are so intimately concerned, that describing it to others becomes a comparatively easy matter and pupils of tender years soon learn to stand without self-consciousness before a large audience and present material accurately, naturally and interestingly.

Less valuable—so it seems to a visitor—are the student councils, which were organized to afford machinery for a limited amount of student self government. Meetings are held weekly and conducted according to the laws of parliamentary procedure. While the older children undoubtedly enjoy and benefit from them, the councils decidedly bear the impress of an adult conceived and adult imposed activity. During the past year the practice was fortunately abandoned of requiring minutes and attendance of delegates from the first three grades.

It is to be expected that as the Lincoln School experiment develops, other reasonable modifications will be made in accordance with the requirements of child interest and growth. Up to the present, the main emphasis of the school has been upon scientific curriculum making, to evolve a curriculum more closely related to the needs of modern society. While certain of the elementary grades are experimenting with free activity, there

are many teachers on the staff who insist that
there must be a known goal and systematic direction of the child's growth towards that goal.
To quote Dr. Rugg once more: ". . . if growth
is to be properly directed, the curriculum maker
must be oriented so as to have his eyes set constantly on the society into which the child is growing."

In accordance with this ideal, no pains and no
expense have been spared to provide the children
with the proper setting. The building of the
Lincoln School is in itself a kind of testimonial
to that great and orderly society in which its
pupils may be expected to play a leading rôle.
The halls are of marble, and of noble proportions.
In them under glass, are many exhibits of the
children's work. The science laboratories are
equipped with the latest and most modern apparatus. There are splendid swimming pools, gymna-
sia, yard and roof playgrounds. Intimacy, which
some people feel is a first requisite for child development, is of course gone, save as it can be
retained by certain more gifted teachers in their
classrooms. The school has an institutional
flavor in common with the Ethical Culture and
Horace Mann Schools, and in common also with
the public schools throughout the country, which
it was organized to serve. Yet much that goes

on within the walls of the Lincoln institution is
liberating. It is of vital importance to cut away
the dead wood of a course of study and start out
with fresh modern material. But curricular reform, after all, is only a fractional part of educational progress. The human spirit is not fed
by mental pabulum alone, even the best that can
be devised. It has a way of eluding even the
worst. The great experiment of the Lincoln
School remains yet to be made, that of studying
and watching the growth and development of children under conditions of real—not institutional
—freedom.

X

FOLLOWING THE CHILD'S LEAD

I

At its annual meeting in 1924 an ambitious proposal was made by the Teachers Union of New York. Following an intensive study of the leading private experimental schools in and near the city, the union has prepared and submitted to the city board of education a scheme for establishing a similar experimental center in the public-school system. The proposal deserves particular consideration because it comes not from outsiders but from a group of workers who have labored long to apply the ordinary methods of instruction. These methods, according to the union, have brought public-school education to a condition of stagnation. Children are turned into automatons by the artificial discipline of drill as an end in itself; they are robbed of their childhood by having to conform to adult standards of thought and behavior; their individual and creative tendencies are smothered by the rigid curriculum to which all must submit; they soon develop antagonistic attitudes toward their work, toward their teacher, their associates, and life in general.

In the school which the union seeks to have established "the boys and girls will reconstruct their experiences in a boys' or girls' world. . . . The environment will be such as to liberate and organize their capacities through self-initiated, self-directed, whole-hearted, purposeful activities. In this way they will be able to experience the sheer joy of living. The curriculum will be as varied, rich, and fluid as life itself." The union observes that in experimental schools conducted on this basis children learn the "fundamentals"—the three R's—better than under the traditional methods. This has been determined by the use of objective standardized tests. The many other gains made by the children become apparent if one makes the slightest examination of what these newer schools have to offer.

The experimental centers which served as models for the union's program included the City and Country School and the Walden School in New York City. The City and Country School was founded (as the Play School) by Caroline Pratt in 1914. The Walden School was started by Margaret Naumburg in 1916 and is now directed by Margaret Pollitzer and Elizabeth Goldsmith. To the extent that they serve to revitalize and raise the standard of public-school procedure, these schools have a significance far beyond the education of the limited number of children who attend them.

In both schools, questions relating to curriculum are of secondary consideration and emphasis is laid upon the child's present needs and his innate capacities and interests. The outstanding purpose is to help the children to evolve a world of their own in which they will think, act, and express themselves on their own level. Book learning as an end is discouraged, especially in the early years, for it represents at best vicarious experiences. Instead, children are given every opportunity to obtain first-hand contact with the world about them and are given ample and varied materials with which to express their own fresh reactions to these contacts. This involves, of course, the abandonment of fixed recitation periods, of assigned lessons, of immovable desks and immovable children. Freedom from constraint, however, does not mean that the pupils "run wild." Indeed, they hold to their self-chosen tasks with a concentration and absorption rarely found in the ordinary schoolroom, where the slightest interruption—the flapping of a blind or the creaking of a door—is sufficient to shift the whole base of the attention of the class. To those inured to the stereotyped and poverty-stricken responses of children brought up in the conventional environment, the creative achievement of the pupils of these newer schools seems almost incredible. This is most dramatically evident in the field of the plastic arts, where the work in drawing, painting, and pottery achieves a standard of high professional merit. Striking work is done in music, in rhythm, and in imaginative writing.

Characteristic of these schools are the lengthening of the school day and the extension of the school's influence to the earliest years of childhood. With the growing recognition on the part of psychologists, physicians, and child-welfare workers generally of the supreme importance of infancy and earliest childhood, nursery schools have been established in many centers which are concerned with studying early growth and habit formation and making certain that they proceed along wholesome lines. The Walden school admits babies as soon as they can walk, and the Nursery School of the New York Bureau of Educational Experiments "graduates" its youngsters into Miss Pratt's school when they reach the age of three. Both schools also maintain a careful and scientific system of record-keeping, covering every possible detail of procedure and of individual and social development. Since the schools are experimental these records are invaluable as means of checking achievement, as well as for the light they shed on hitherto unexplored fields of child growth.

While the two schools have thus much in common, their method of approach is very different. In so far as classification is possible for either, it may be said that the City and Country School has been influenced by the teaching of behaviorist psychology and the Walden School by that of analytic psychology. Now the psychologist who is concerned chiefly with the science of human behavior declares that the individual can be trained to withstand most of the shocks and disasters of life by being properly "conditioned" in early childhood—by having the right instead of the wrong sensory stimuli presented to him and acquiring early the proper habits of response. The analytic psychologist is also concerned with childhood, but chiefly because of the mechanism of the unconscious to which he believes are relegated the unpleasant incidents of life, especially those of early youth.

Now, it will not do to draw any fine psychological distinctions between the City and Country and Walden schools, but in general terms it might be

·said that the former is interested in what children do, how they act, and what use they make of their environment, whereas the latter school is mostly concerned with underlying motive and emotional make-up. This does not mean that one school hopes to develop objective and the other subjective types of people, nor that in one school children will grow up mainly interested in materials and in the other mainly interested in introspective and personal relationships, but the differences between the two schools have this general trend.

Miss Pratt's behaviorist "slant" is well shown in these sentences from her book on the City and Country School, published by E. P. Dutton:

We are not willing to be dominated or have the children dominated by subject matter. We wish them to form strong habits of first-hand research and to use what they find; we want them to discover relationships in concrete matter so that they will know that they exist when they deal with abstract forms. We want them to have a fine motor experience because they themselves are motor and to get and retain what they get through bodily perceptions.

Miss Pratt has developed her curriculum very much more completely than has the Walden School. As the result of ten years' testing of her

theories she is now prepared to assert that certain
activities are better performed at certain age levels
than at others. For example, seven-year-old children in her school always have for their main
enterprise for the year the building of a miniature city in permanent form, just as at six they
reproduce the city in block form. At seven, the
children construct wooden houses, which they
paint, furnish, and wire, they lay out streets, trol-
ley lines, and waterways with a full quota of boats.
At eight, the children run the supply store for the
school, taking complete charge of all orders and
accounting for the money. While not an advocate of formal programs, Miss Pratt believes that
the programs of successive years should bear definite relationship to one another and that one year's
activities should grow naturally from those of
the years preceding. At seven, she also has the
children begin their work in reading, writing, and
arithmetic. Before that age is reached they have
acquired some number sense and a limited ability
to recognize written symbols. But at seven, she
has discovered, they become more concerned with
realities, their drive becomes more conscious, they
emerge from the merely play world, and desire to
be taught. To those who have made a fetish of
sugar-coating the three R's, the story of one
youngster is instructive. She reported enthusi-

astically to her mother one day that spelling was her favorite subject. When her mother inquired whether that was because of some new way of teaching it the child replied: "Oh, no, Miss —— just says *do* it, and we do it!"

When standard achievement tests are applied, Miss Pratt's children always show up extremely well in the formal subjects. In the record of the eight-year-old group appended to this chapter are the scores attained in reading and arithmetic. Only two of the class fell below the level for their age; four read as well as ten-year-old children; two as well as eleven years old, and one as well as thirteen years. The arithmetic scores were not quite as superior because the business of store keeping had caused the children to mark off two decimal places, where none belonged. Every child however was up to grade, and seven ranged from one to three grades ahead. A recent comparison of problems solved by Miss Pratt's children and those of a very efficient demonstration school, showed that Miss Pratt's children excelled in originality in ways of problem solving, but fell somewhat below in speed and accuracy. During the winter of 1924-25 a special arithmetic teacher was appointed to be on the lookout for opportunities for teaching necessary arithmetic to help children do better the activities they have initiated.

One boy for instance, failed after many weeks of work to make the motor in his toy motor boat function (both motor and boat were constructed by him in the school shop). His failure was due to faulty arithmetic in making calculations.

Miss Pratt's attitude towards the results of the tests is illuminating: "They prove the teacher's ability to train these youngsters in the specific things they will have to know in carrying out a future program. They have little to do with the education of the children. . . . A person is trained by another, but he educates himself. If we could once get that idea into the consciousness of our parenthood and our teacherhood, the revolution in our school procedure would be immediate." [1]

Opportunities for this self-education are everywhere present. "Information" which the traditional school holds so dear, is acquired naturally as the children carry on their enterprises. Miss Stott's record amply proves this. The coveted post of cashier or messenger in the group store could not be held by children unable to perform the necessary operations in arithmetic. Geography may be said to start with the three and four year olds. The little ones learn to go about the

[1] "Experimental Practice in the City and Country School," by Caroline Pratt, E. P. Dutton, 1924.

school and to locate their room with reference to the rest of the building. Later they venture out into the streets and locate the school. Excursions to parks, markets, docks, bridges, public buildings broaden their knowledge of their immediate world and furnish material for reconstruction in block, clay, story, or pictorial form. Their inquiries about everything with which they come into contact leads to their acquiring an immense amount of information not found in textbooks. Miss Pratt is far less interested in having the children learn the States of the Union and their capitals than to have them discover the interrelation of different parts of trade and industry and our dependence upon them. "In building a body of what the schools call 'general information' unrelated to the child's experience, they build of straw." The six-year-old group who paid repeated visits to a Cuban steamer each time it docked accumulated a vivid store of material about Cuba which formal instruction would never have provided.

There are, of course, certain matters in Miss Pratt's school about which perhaps more discussion is needed. It is possible that under less wise leadership Miss Pratt's insistence upon program-making might result in too great formalism. One might also question whether the very complete classification of children by chronological age and the formulating of activities according to varying age levels is not injecting something at once spurious and artificial. The intelligence testers have made us all sensitive to the question of "age," but obviously a child is an individual first and a given age second, and it is as an individual with his abilities and disabilities that he has first claim on our attention. Advances in analytic psychology may also modify Miss Pratt's very emphatic contention that there is something "unfortunate" about a child who does not "attack" materials, but instead has his interest "riveted" in people.

Miss Pratt has also been occasionally criticized for limiting the development of imagination by keeping the children too much in the present and giving them too much concrete material. Her answer is that the first-hand experiences of children contain the factual elements necessary to art. "Vivid auditory and perceptive images come from vivid experiences." Children who can observe deeply, whose interests are kept alive, and who remain sensitive to new impressions cannot be lacking in imaginative power. As a matter of fact, the imaginative plays, drawings, and writings of the older groups in the school are of a high order. The twelve-year-old class has recently given a performance of Euripides's "Alcestis" which would do credit to maturer students. Their back-drop and costumes, their original music played on lyres made in the school-shop were delightfully executed. There is, thinks Miss Pratt, too much vicarious living, too much vicarious enjoyment in our civilization. Children if taken young enough and helped to develop their own creative purposes will establish habits of being motivated from within, which is the only way in which original and artistic work can be achieved.

II

The following record was written by the group teacher, Miss Leila V. Stott, of the activities of the eight-year-old children for the month of April, 1924. It is preceded by a few paragraphs from the October record bearing on the beginning of the store, which as has been already indicated, is the central activity of the year.

The record has value in many ways. It answers specifically at least for the group and the month covered, the question, what kind of things go on in an experimental school? It also shows how fruitfully the interests of children lead to worth while activities not only in dramatization, music, dancing, painting, pottery or music, but in the more formal fields of reading, writing, number work, geography and history, as well.

EXCERPTS FROM THE RECORD OF
GROUP VIII

From the October, 1924, record.

THE STORE

The group came to school prepared to undertake the business of running a stationery store, as last year's VIII's did, to sell supplies to other school groups. They had already met with last year's class, last spring, and agreed to buy the stock left over as well as certain store fixtures such as shelves and counter. There was some discussion about this as some of the children wanted to make their own fixtures, but others thought it important to have the store ready to open as soon as possible. This view prevailed so it was decided to buy all the supplies offered. The group borrowed $50 from the school office as capital and gave a promissory note in return. Their first business on returning to school was the taking of an inventory to check up the supplies found in the store with the list left by last year's class. The various items as reported by the children were written for them on the board and copied by each child in order to have individual copies of the whole inventory. Several suggestions were made for improving the store equipment, including a plan for a better show case. Mr. Reber was called in for consultation and time in the shop arranged for. After discussion of all the preparations necessary, it was decided to open the store on Monday, the 8th, and letters announcing the opening were written and sent to all the classes in the school. Several posters were also started, but only Vera's was finished in time and posted on the store door. Two trips were taken to get prices and supplies found to be needed and the group also had a call from a salesman who wanted to supply our needs. We gave him samples and asked him to submit prices. It was found we would need certain class supplies like pencils and account books preliminary to opening the store, so we drew from the school office, $10 for our October allowance and opened the store for a private sale. This necessitated opening books for the store and for the class, and the first treasurers and bookkeepers were chosen by me for their facility in the necessary techniques. We decided to choose each week a class treasurer, sales bookkeeper and expense bookkeeper so that all might share in the experience. All the group practiced writing sales slips, writing columns of price numbers from dictation and adding.

When the store opened on October 8th, the class was divided into five committees of three each, one committee to have charge of the store each day so that every child served once a week.

A student teacher helped in the store during the first two weeks. Each Friday the books are balanced. The class book is taken because it is simple and the class writes the totals from this dictation and adds. Results are compared and corrections made where necessary. The treasurer then announces the amount received at the beginning of the week and each child calculates by counting up from total spent the amount that should be in the cash box. Leonard who was first class treasurer, on finding himself two pennies short, decided at once to make a new cash box as the one left us by last year's class had cracks. He produced a box admired by all for its fine workmanship.

After the class accounts are settled, the store books are attacked in the same way, the bookkeepers reading the totals for each day and the rest adding individually. When different results are reported, all go over the work to discover which is right until unanimity is reached. The subtraction of the expense total from the amount received is done by me on the board and explained, but the children often calculate the difference mentally by counting up from expense total to total receipts. Counting of the actual cash at the end of the first week revealed the serious deficit of $4.90. This was discussed by all and as the box had been carefully padlocked the possibility of theft was dismissed, and carelessness in making change or making entries in the book was held responsible. As one instance was known where $1.00 too much had been given in change and returned by a teacher, this seemed a probable explanation and pointed to the necessity for more practice in making change.

The new show case was finished and equipped with an electric light by Walter with help from Herbert, the new paper rack was finished by Walter and the girls took much pleasure in arranging the stocks and putting on the price labels.

Every one wrote an individual price list from a copy I put on the board and the two lists easiest to read were posted in the store. Prices of goods bought from last year's class were taken from their price list and new goods bought by us were marked at the usual retail price. Tables of crayon prices (.02) up to a dozen were posted in the store and also prices for large drawing paper (.03 a sheet), erasers (.05), pads (.06) and pencils (.07). As only the 2 table is universally known, these lists are important aids to salesmen. All the classes have been asked to order ahead by mail in order to avoid delays in the store and the reading of the daily business mail is an important part of the morning business meeting. It has brought out a decided preference for print over script writing. Business letters have been written to outside firms by Herbert and Alice and have brought answers and the supplies ordered.

The election of bookkeepers has brought out the need for a test of capacity. Leonard questioned Nell's fitness on the ground that she used "scribbly writing." Nell claimed to be able to write in print, too, and Leonard demanded evidence before voting. Both candidates were asked to do some specimen writing on the board and the class voted with the evidence before them.

The trimming of the show case, cleaning up of the store each day, arrangement of stock, the counting of money in the cash box, have all been full of real play interest.

RECORD FOR APRIL, 1924

I. *Play Experiences*

ORGANIZED GAMES

There has been a great development of interest in baseball this month. Walter, Edna and

Margery are the leading spirits and have practiced alone when there were not enough players
for a real game, but with the encouragement from
me the whole class has joined in the enthusiasm
and has divided into two sides headed respectively
by Margery and Walter for daily practice. Jason,
in spite of interest in the game has been so di-
verted by the attraction of play in the "river
yard," that he did not give much time to base
ball until, by Miss Pratt's advice, I announced
that the river yard would be open to Group VIII
only during the noon and after school session.
This new ruling brought Leonard and Harry also
into the regular baseball practice and although
these two did not so obviously need the discipline
of organized games as Jason, it is making for a
better group spirit to have their interest keen in
the games. As both these boys stay for the
after school time, they are not losing their opportunity for the quieter kind of dramatic play
with trains. Next to Margery, Alice has become most enthusiastic of all the girls over baseball, but Vera and Emma play regularly, and Vera
and Jane are considered better players than Alice.
Grace and Bertha were also considered valuable
assets to a team, but have been absent so much
that they have had little practice this month.
Vera usually announces she is not going to play,

but when this is accepted without comment, changes her mind and asks for a place in the game. Nell and Elizabeth like to play, but dread the criticism of the others as neither succeeds in batting the ball at all. Walter, as captain of one side, has shown real interest in coaching Elizabeth and does it in a very nice spirit. Ellis finds it hard to see himself in the unusual position of being excelled by Walter and Margery, but takes this salutary experience well with only occasional longings for soccer instead of baseball. Walter, Jason, Margery and Alice were raised into seventh heaven one day by being taken into a practice game of the XII's.

There has also been some basket ball practice in the gymnasium on rainy days, especially by Walter, Harry, Jane, Elsa and Margery. Nell, Elizabeth and Grace still cling exclusively to the rings.

PLAY WITH BIG MATERIALS

The first time the "Covered Wagon" play was taken up again after vacation, the children found themselves so hopelessly stale on it that they agreed with relief to my suggestion to drop it. Later on, however, interest revived among the girls, and there seemed to be a feeling of incompletion after all the work on costumes, so the whole group discussed the situation and agreed to give the play but to make certain changes in parts. All the boys and Alice wanted to make changes and the boys also suggested a new Indian scene in an Iroquois Long House. Jason, Harry and Leonard dressed up as Indians and worked out spontaneously a very good pantomime of departure on a deer hunt and return with a deer. This was, of course, suggested by the original Indian play they made up earlier in the year, but Leonard added details drawn from the story of Apauk which he has been re-reading alone, dealing with the Indian's fast and dream in order to get "good medicine" for the hunt.

MAP MAKING

The introduction of some plasticine the last week of the month led to a wave of enthusiasm for making relief maps. The first maps were of the Hudson and Mohawk valleys with Catskill and Adirondack Mountains, and including Lakes George and Champlain and sometimes the Green Mountains beyond. The divides between the Hudson Valley and Lake Champlain and between the Mohawk and the Oswego Rivers were always indicated though the latter river is not known by name.

No two maps of course are exactly alike, but nearly all begin from the northern end of Manhattan and show the Palisades. Fort Orange, or Albany, as it is called interchangeably, is also indicated on these maps and sometimes part of Lake Erie and some of the New York State Lakes. Streams flowing into the Hudson and Mohawk feature in all maps and all water is painted blue. Walter also made a map of Manhattan and the surrounding territory including Staten Island, Long Island, the Sound and Upper Bay and marked subway routes and bridges to Brooklyn. Nell and Elizabeth followed suit. Ellis, Jason and Harry branched out into maps of South America featuring the Andes and the Amazon River with Para at its mouth. Nearly every one took up this idea next, rejoicing over the easy coast line of South America as compared with the irregularities of North America. Consultation of maps resulted in the spontaneous addition of the La Plata River and the Brazilian Highlands and the location of Buenos Aires, Rio de Janeiro and the cattle ranches of Brazil. The accidental leaving of a strip of low land west of the Andes on Vera's map led to my recognition of it as Chile, and it now appears on all maps. Emma had heard of the A. B. C. republics so I explained the three names and showed how they belonged roughly to these three divisions that appear on their maps. Cape Horn and the Panama Canal are universally featured. Harry made the most beautiful map of all and adorned it with such significant symbols as a cow on the Brazilian highland, a steamer on an indicated course from Buenos Aires (where it got meat) to Para (for rubber), and off Cape Horn, a mast schooner. Jason, on the other hand, objects to all such play symbols and wants a "real map." Both he and Walter have shown a more sustained and concentrated interest in this than any other activity except store and baseball. With the exception of the store and dramatics, no other activity has been shared so completely by the whole group, girls and boys alike, as this map making. Clay has been used when the supply of plasticine gave out, but is unsatisfactory for permanent results.

DRAWING AND PAINTING

Leonard was still eager to draw when he first came back after the holidays, but talked so much he could accomplish nothing. I therefore insisted on his drawing alone in the store if he wanted to

draw at all. He protested violently at first, but
the results were so good that he became interested
and soon took voluntarily to the store, asking to
have the door closed to insure greater quiet. Later
on however a new enthusiasm for reading relegated drawing for the first time to a very subor-
dinate position. The forest scenery for the play
was finished by him with the assistance of Jane,
Margery, Jason and Harry, but the only real
enthusiasm for drawing this month has been on
the part of Nell, Elizabeth, Emma, Vera and
Elise who worked all the first two weeks whenever
they had a chance on the interiors of houses.
Nell's results were particularly good as in her ex-
teriors of last month and she started the fashion
of pasting her pictures together in long suites of
rooms to make up a whole house plan. Mr. Zorach was much interested in these designs of hers
when he came in one day for a special painting
period. I had asked him to come in because I
felt that Leonard and Ellis and Jason were rather
at a standstill in their drawing and painting and
perhaps needed help in technique, and all the
children needed some stimulus toward a bolder
and freer use of their materials. Leonard had
already started on a large painting of a scene in
the interior of a Log House inspired by his plan
for the new act in the play and Mr. Zorach's en-

couragement gave him new inspiration. Ellis responded, too, with a large scale painting of a bear followed by one of the Amazon jungle. He consulted pictures of palm trees for details in this latter picture and asked me many questions too about the kinds of growth and the animals to be found there.

Mr. Zorach admired a color effect Emma had produced in a small painting and asked her to repeat it on a large scale which she did very successfully in the first large painting she has made this year. Alice attempted a large scale drawing of an Indian with his Long House in the background, but was dissatisfied with it and unwilling to finish it. Walter has done two large crayon drawings, one a map begun by Leonard and turned over to Walter at the latter's request, and the second a very good ship coming head on, probably copied from one of Ellis' on the wall. It showed, however, great improvement in technique and a gain in confidence as well. The week before Easter was marked by a passion for making Easter cards on the part of five girls. They made them on order for other children as well as for themselves. The same kind of work on decorative designs, small scale illustrations and illuminated letters has gone into much of their making of books.

POTTERY AND CLAY MODELING

Much less time than formerly has been spent by the girls in this kind of work, but Nell has produced a very good tea pot which has been fired and she has finished and glazed a pitcher and sugar bowl as well. Jane spent a good deal of time working alone one week when drops in her eyes prevented her from joining many other kinds of work, and she made a life size rabbit which she painted and took home for an Easter present. She also made a grotesque head which she decided to name the Hunch Back of Notre Dame. Ellis has done a good deal of modeling, always of animals. His white seal, inspired by Kipling's story, and a model of a python strangling a deer particularly show a stirring of the imagination as well as remarkable technique.

II. *Practical Experience*

STORE

Interest holds so universally that there is a strong protest from the store committee against taking trips in the morning and missing store time. Twice, however, this protest has been met by the agreement to let the committee that lost its turn substitute for absent members of other committees and volunteers from Group IX have kept store for us so that we could have extra time for trips. Jason asks regularly to have special number work given him in free time or at home so that he can act as special messenger for the store when needed. Leonard continues enthusiastic about all bookkeeping and cashier work and is very accurate in adding long columns, sometimes saving sales slips for two days to enter all at once in order to get a longer column to add. He was absent the last day before book balancing, so I asked for a volunteer to get the books written up to date, and Walter responded not so much from interest in the job as from realization that it had to be done before the books could be balanced. Nell, who is better than most of the group in the technique of arithmetic (familiarity with combinations, tables, etc.), still becomes easily confused in actual store work, cannot balance her accounts as cashier without help and has difficulty counting out the right amount of change, though she readily calculates in her head the amount needed. Bertha, on the other hand, was so clear in her thinking that when she found the cash in the box 2 cents short of the amount shown by her book, she at once put her finger on the difficulty by admitting she had changed one sales slip from 10 cents to 12 cents because she thought the wrong price had been charged. She produced the slip on which she had made a note of her correction. Mistakes in spelling on sales slips are usually noted by all bookkeepers and the slips are given back to the person responsible, to be corrected.

SHOP

Walter and Jane finally finished the cashier's cage and installed it in the store amid universal approval. It consists of three frames covered with chicken wire and fastened together with hinges so that it surrounds the cashier's table on three sides. It has, of course, a window in front through which money is handed in and out. Emma and Vera finished the frame for scenery and have mounted the latter. Walter and Ellis both made swords—for no school purpose—and Walter continues to work on his aeroplane which is an ambitious undertaking. Ellis has made a Greek ship following a design found in a book of ships. The inspiration came from the story of the "Children's Homer," which Mr. Paley is reading aloud at rest time. Harry and Jason have both worked on boats for use in the river yard. Harry's has a tin keel, a mast, and many fine details as is characteristic of all his work.

The girls' work in the shop has been chiefly on stilts and all of them are now provided with gayly painted sets. Elizabeth and Nell are at work now on bird houses for use in the country and are doing careful work with intense concentration. Mr. Reber reports that Ellis is lacking in independence in working on his Greek ship. I asked a student teacher to report on Walter's work in shop when he went by special arrangement at 9.30 one day, and she reported such splendid concentration, in spite of fooling going on by several older boys in Mr. Reber's absence, that he has been allowed to go often at this time when Mr. Reber could be there.

GROUP MANAGEMENT

By accident I came in late one afternoon without previous notice and found the children gathered in a reading circle according to the program I had put on the board. Emma was reading aloud Tappan's "Colonial Stories." On the whole there has been much less restlessness and better concentration since the return to regular programs. Free program making is now confined to Fridays after book balancing is over and is much enjoyed, though actual changes in the program are few. Walter and Jason get in extra shop periods usually on these free days, Leonard and Bertha and Alice read more and all do more drawing or typewriting.

CARE OF ROOM AND MATERIALS

Jason has taken charge of the paints and brushes and keeps the cloths washed. Leonard volunteered to assist him and serve in his absence, and I rarely have to take any responsibility about this now. There is also great improvement in leaving tables picked up before going to yard or lunch. Emma and Vera one day volunteered to scrub the floor on which some paint had been spilled, and enjoyed the job so much that they proceeded to give the store a thorough cleaning, too. One week when Vera was class treasurer she discovered that the treasury was down to 17 cents and we had only one roll of paper towelling left, so by careful watching and frequent urging of economical use she made the towel last two weeks!

III. *Special Training*

DANCING

The return to "regular dancing" after the time spent on dramatics has been enjoyed by all. Jason still protests at times, but is interested when actually at work. Elizabeth and Nell seem to have been released by the dramatic play to a very marked extent and show freedom and original thinking as well as good listening in fitting patterns and pantomime to music. One period was spent in a square dance with spontaneously evolved figures. All tried out figures and Miss Doing chose several good ones to be tried out by the whole group. There was great enthusiasm over this especially on part of the girls, but no one has wanted to try it again.

The usual stretching exercises, cart wheels and standing on hands have occupied all the time not spent on dancing patterns and pantomimes. Jason and Ellis continue to ask regularly for the cowboy play, but only once has the rest of the group joined in the request and secured the opportunity.

All the boys are improving in cart wheels, but only Walter as yet can stand on his hands, and none of the boys approach Margery and Emma or any of the girls except Nell and Elizabeth in agility. Jane, as usual, shows keenest ability to fit her movements to the music as was especially shown in dancing alone to music which had two well marked voices and was danced by most of the children in couples, each partner choosing one voice to follow. Jane followed one voice with her feet and another with hand movements. All the boys have improved in seriousness of work and in adjusting to the music.

MUSIC

There has been a good spirit of serious work and real interest in the music all the month. Ellis and Leonard have become so interested in playing on the marimbas now that they have started to make their own at last. The last month had included a good deal of singing of familiar songs for pleasure, especially quiet songs conducive to good tone in order to counteract the over excitement evidenced by rough tone and constant interruptions, also a good deal of band work which involved accurate listening and watching the director. Besides this kind of work there had been a good deal of straight technique such as drill in singing notes of the scale from hand signs, and this month all of this seemed to bear fruit in better tone, alertness and interest so a few new songs were introduced and learned readily. Practice in recognizing songs is a part of each lesson. "Human marimbas," made by numbering the children up to five and making tunes by calling on each child to sing his own number as indicated by the teacher, is a very entertaining game. "Spelling" tunes sung by teacher is another new game and is done by singing back the same air giving numbers instead of syllables "la" sung by teacher.

One lesson was skipped because the group begged to go out to see a match game in the yard, and Miss Hubbell did not want them to come to music under compulsion. Jane, Bertha and Emma were unwilling to lose the music period and stayed for free work with marimbas, numbers read from staff and the big drum. Two tunes were now played on marimbas and followed pretty well by all but Walter and Jason, who became confused in playing with the group. There has been special drill on holding the long notes in phrases. Drill on distinguishing between major and minor chords aroused interest, but proved still too difficult for most of the children. Walter, Herbert and Vera never made a mistake in this. Harry asked many questions, but did not actually listen accurately. Nell's steady improvement throughout the year has been very noticeable. Last year she rarely entered into group singing, seldom gave individual responses, and her inability to listen made her pitch very inaccurate. Now she sings with well shaped mouth for words, her pitch is much steadier and her better attention and concentration together with a longer span of interest makes her responses to technical questions much more intelligent.

Jason, because of serious objection to music, was dropped from group work and allowed to spend the music period in special number work. He was given the weekly half hour of free time with Miss Hubbell instead of group work and improved so much in interest and technique that he returned to the group at his own request at the end of the month.

NUMBER

Drill on the multiplication tables needed in store work, i.e., 2, 3, 5 and 6 tables, has taken up much time and interest. Most of the children have also learned the 4 table, and Ellis, Jason, Walter and Alice went on with the 7. The method of learning them is to make the tables for themselves by addition, to test each other in couples and then come to me for a final test. I give multiplication and short division examples on the table learned. Leonard always does better in the actual examples than in abstract drill questions. This work is usually done during store time by those not serving in the store itself. Jason has taken home examples to do or has done them in school free time in order to be allowed extra service in the store as special messenger. Walter still writes 16 in place of 61, etc. Occasionally Vera, too, makes this mistake even in copying from the board.

Alice asked for number work to do in free time one day and I started her and Emma working problems from an Arithmetic book. Walter came in and asked to do the same kind next day. Since then a craze for book work has spread through the class, with the exception of Jane, Jason and Leonard. Problems "with reading" are specially sought and done very readily as the technical difficulties are slight.

Drawing the plan of a house to the scale of 8 feet to an inch proved very interesting and the dimensions of the whole house and of each room were found by translating the measured inches to feet. The question of area arose in this connection for both Herbert and Vera and they easily caught on to the process of multiplying length by width to obtain square feet after I drew out some square feet to show what was meant by this term. Alice is particularly fond of mental arithmetic games which she often starts. Drill on the tables has led to practice in taking fractional parts of numbers, too, and this often enters into the mental arithmetic games, but usually causes several children to drop out.

Subtraction that involves borrowing still has difficulties for most of the group. Only Alice, Emma, Herbert and Grace never ask for help.

WRITING AND SPELLING

A craze for writing stories by all the girls followed the introduction of a regular writing period twice a week. Jason, Harry and Walter, who dictated to me a fine cowboy story, were very willing to start copying it into their books, but needed pressure to get it done. Walter has done very good writing when he works alone in the store and is improving. He takes pleasure in a neat looking page, and so does Jason. Herbert writes easily and willingly, composing original stories. Leonard still writes beautifully but laboriously, and escapes to the typewriter if I let him. I announced as a general rule that first choice of the typewriter would be given those who had a good handwritten copy with correct spelling and sentence formations and this has helped to relieve the pressure. Spelling shows improvement in familiarity with frequently recurring syllables like "er, tle, sion, ing," etc., and I can answer questions as to spelling often by simply referring to other similar words (i.e., spell "light" like "night"). Bertha, Emma, Harry and Alice are

recognized as authorities and appealed to when I
am not available.

READING

See list of books appended at end of notes.

Jason and Leonard came back after the holidays eager for a new Indian book to read. I
gave them "Dokos," but they did not take to it as
well as to "Red Feather." Walter brought a
"Book of Cowboys" to school and read it steadily
with enthusiasm though it was written in adult
style. He followed this with "Buffalo Bill's
Boyhood." Margery has now started on "Red
Feather II" and reads it alone in free time as well
as in the regular reading period. Unfortunately
her ability to gather the content of a story without
knowing the actual words makes it possible for
her to get enjoyment without accuracy and she
feels no need of assistance and resists reading
aloud to me. She, Elizabeth and Jason are now
the only ones who need special help, and Elizabeth
and Jason are glad to read with me or a student
teacher.

About the middle of the month, Leonard suddenly developed a reading enthusiasm that has
quite launched him into ability to read any kind
of material that interests him. He began by read-

ing the "Cliff Dwellers" through at a sitting.
(Jason, too, started this but broke his glasses and
Nell finished it aloud for him.)   This, Leonard
followed by "Mewanee," also read straight
through regardless of yard time, which I let him
miss because it was a day on which we had dancing involving lively physical exercises.   From
"Mewanee" he went to "Apauk," an Indian story
I had read aloud to the group earlier and had
found so adult in style that I had skipped a good
deal in reading aloud.   He read this with the
same absorption and utilized parts of it in our
play.   His surprise in his own enjoyment of reading was amusing.   The "Lake Dwellers," too, he
finished at one sitting.   He has also read part of
Baldwin's "Explorers of the Northwest," as have
Harry, Nell and Emma.   Jane had been reading
the "Just So Stories" and "My Book House," and
I feared both were too hard for her, so asked her
several times to read to me so I could check up
on it, but she always succeeded in convincing me
she could read the stories she had chosen.

LANGUAGE

The girls were all absorbed in writing stories
which had so little sign of interest in pattern or
sense impressions that I called the group together

one day for discussion of stories and suggested trying to make pictures in words as they did on paper. I proposed as illustration that some one dictate a short story that would make us feel like winter, and another about summer. Margery quickly responded but all the girls were eager to go on with their writing and had no desire to dictate. Walter, Harry and Jason, however, stayed with me to dictate a vivid cowboy story which interested them so much that they were quite willing to copy it into books of their own. Herbert wrote for himself a story of the same type to go into his "Book of Western Life," and Leonard began one, but has only reached the middle of the second chapter as yet. Margery's story carried over the impetus I had tried to give toward more vivid expression, but the rest show little sign of it. I think the group needs much more opportunity for dictated stories than I have been giving them.

(See appendix to notes for original stories of this month.)

IV. *Organization of Information*

DISCUSSIONS

At the first meeting after vacation, Jason raised the question of having some school pets, either rabbits or pigeons. There was general approval of the idea, and Jane and Emma undertook to see Miss Pratt about it. She came in next day to our meeting and told of the difficulties of giving the animals the kind of environment that would make them happy, but agreed to letting us have guinea pigs when Emma suggested a place where they could run wild and yet be somewhat protected. She also proposed a salt water aquarium. (None of this has materialized due to the pressure of other interests.)

In connection with the play we have been developing, an outline map of New York was hung up and New York City was identified as a starting point. The Hudson River was then put on in chalk, Fort Orange or Albany, the Mohawk River, Lakes George and Champlain were added by various volunteers and Walter put in the "Great Carry" between Lake Champlain and the Hudson and the Catskill and Adirondack Mountains. I told them there was a level plain around the shore of the Great Lakes and invited speculation as to the reason for this. Leonard and Walter were quick to present theories. Walter thought that soil washed down from the mountains by rain might have fallen into the lakes and formed a level border around the edge, while Leonard recalled that I had said once that the

lakes used to be larger than at present and thought
the border was old lake bottom.   I asked what
might have caused a contraction of the water
surface and he suggested a widening of the opening into the St. Lawrence, so that "more water
went out that way."   The girls listened but could
not be induced to participate at all in the speculation.   They acted timid and self-conscious.

As the play interest was dropped temporarily
after this, I introduced the pencil exhibit sent us
by the Dixon factory and we discussed the origin
of the graphite and cedar wood of which the pencils were made.   As the graphite proved to come
from Ticonderoga on Lake Champlain, a new interest was added to that section of the map.   We
looked for the route by which graphite could be
brought to Jersey City, where the pencil factory
is, and Herbert at once raised the question, "How
do they get across the 'Carry'?"   Trains were
suggested and I told about the Champlain Canal
across the divide.   The necessity of mixing the
graphite with clay led to a discussion of where
this was to be found and Jason told of seeing
it in New Jersey.   Elise and Jane had seen bricks
being made at Kingston on the Hudson, but did
not know they had any connection with clay.
Harry reported seeing red clay and this led to a
discussion of iron in the soil.   Walter told of

seeing old iron mines and Elise and Jane had seen
them, too. Some one, I think Vera, said glue was
used to put the two halves of a pencil together and
where did that come from? Tom, therefore, invited us to visit his grandfather's glue factory.
(See trips.)

In the discussion which followed this trip Vera
took a leading part. Her interest was especially
keen in the "old streets" we had seen in the neighborhood of Pecks Slip and their associations with
the first Dutch settlers we have read about.
Front Street, which we had read was filled in by
settlers and which we had found now two blocks
from the water front, raised the question of how
sand was washed in by the sea in some places and
taken away in others. Vera's question, "How can
you build on sand?" was answered by the boys,
"You drive down to rock underneath." Vera
persisted, however, in asking, "How can you drive
into water?" and this led to reference to bridge
supports and tubes under the river with constant
recalling of building operations seen in the city.

Herbert and Walter, who had stayed home from
the trip to make pencil leads of graphite in the
laboratory, described their experience and showed
the result. They said the lead broke very easily
and I asked if any one had any idea about what
is done to harden it. Jane suggested putting it

in the sun, with a reference in her mind I think to the hardening of clay in that way. As heat is really the answer to the problem this made a good introduction.

The trip experiences also brought out the connection between glue and gelatin which we saw being prepared at the factory and the relation between glue and glove making. This last was due to the fact that the main glue factory is located in the Mohawk Valley near the glove center, in order to utilize the unused bits of bones and hides. The children themselves suggested that the glove factories were originally located there because deer were plentiful and many skins could be had.

The discussion of graphite and other forms of coal was resumed and Emma described its origin from leaves. Herbert said yes and from tree trunks too, upon which there followed a lively discussion of the looks of decaying vegetation and of the prehistoric forests. This once more brought a question of the origin of the first animal and Jason launched forth upon an account of how life developed from one-cell organisms with propagation by budding and fission on to a description of low forms of sea life attached to the ocean floor, like coral, etc. He had acquired this knowledge in Group IX earlier in the year and was very clear about it in his own mind, but I doubted whether he was really getting much over to the rest so stopped his lecture. The next day, however, he was asked to repeat it to the group and held their interest well. Emma brought in some pictures of coral formation to show us.

In connection with the interest in coal we had some lantern slides from the Natural History Museum on coal mining and the children were especially interested in pictures of pieces of coal showing the imprint of leaves. Jane and Margery went home together planning to search their coal cellars for coal with these markings. Further discussions led to a consideration of mining from the point of view of the workers and the dangers and disagreeable features of the work. The length of the working day was counted up to see how early a miner would probably have to leave home and when he would get back, and much interest was shown in the safety devices against gas. Child labor in mines was briefly discussed and the laws against it, and I explained what a "union" means and some of its practical workings outside the wage bargain such as the institution of a check weighman at the mine head. (Vera thought it would be rather risky to trust even a fellow member to oversee this for you.)

After the subject of graphite had been finished,

we returned to the large map of the two hemispheres to trace the route by which cedar wood was brought from Florida to the Jersey City factory. The coral formation of Florida was discussed in connection with the growth of cedar there and climate was also discussed and the different zones of temperature located on the map. By measuring distances, places of corresponding temperature were discovered on the Northern and Southern hemispheres. The Mohawk Valley gap was looked for on this big map which shows altitude in colors and was easily found. I asked why this physical feature was of importance to the trade of New York City and Leonard answered, "Because trains can get through and bring things to sell in New York." I asked if it was used before trains, and "covered wagons." Indians and buffaloes were mentioned as preceding railroads over this trail.

The use of the big map and the discussion of the temperature zones led to interest in South America, so I sent Alice and the boys all into the library with a student teacher one morning to look up books on rubber and report back to us. Meanwhile the rest of the group pursued a discussion of how paint used on pencils was made. This led to coal tar dyes and turpentine and we located the Southern forests where resin is gathered from pine trees and discussed the process and its effect on the forests. The rubber group came back enthusiastic over their discovery uniting in the recommendation of a story Jason had found in Chamberlain's "How We Are Clothed," and I read this story to the whole group. The next day was spent on the trip to a steamer just in from Para with rubber, and several discussions were on points brought out by this trip. The plasticene map making described above (I) also brought out much incidental discussion about South America, the two principal river systems, the location of Para, Manaos (on the Amazon) "Rio" and Buenos Aires, and the mountains "like a wall."

TRIPS

There have been three trips this month: to the Higgins Glue Factory and Fulton Market, to the Natural History Museum to see a model of a mine working and some specimens of coal with leaves imprinted on them, and to Booth Steamship Co. docks at the Bush Terminal, at 33d Street, Brooklyn, to see a steamer in from Para with a cargo of rubber.

The chief interest at the factory seemed to be in the machinery itself and in the laboratory where products were tested. Jason was particularly thrilled over this process and all saw very clearly exactly how the tests were made and for what purpose. A visit was also paid to the fleet of small fishing schooners at Fulton Market. The men on the docks and at the fish stalls talked to us about their fishing experiences.

The Museum trip proved one of the most stimulating and satisfactory we have had because of the great interest in coal and fossil imprints. The children themselves discovered the most interesting exhibits and showed them to me.

The event of the month, however, was the trip to the ship from Para. The docks were full of hams of crude rubber and hills of Brazil nuts with which the children were invited to fill their pockets. An officer took us all over the ship, including a trip to the engine room, where we talked with engineers and stokers, saw the coal bunkers, the instrument by which the orders are received from the captain on the bridge, the machine which makes salt water fresh and all the workings of the ship. Maps of the Amazon and the ship's course were eagerly studied and many questions asked about how wide the river was and how far the ship could go.

STORIES

Kipling's story of the White Seal led to requests for more "from that book," and we read the story of Mowgli which brought insistent requests for the "Second Jungle Book." Jason asked, "Who ever wrote such a good story," which is the first time I have ever heard a spontaneous question about authorship from any one in the group. Mrs. Mitchell's story about the invention of the first pencil was also enthusiastically received as was the story of rubber from "How We Are Clothed."

LABORATORY EXPERIMENTATION

Walter and Herbert made pencil leads of graphite by mixing powder with water and working the soft mixture into a glass tube as a mold. Most of the groups followed their example and tried the same experiment.

Another day, Walter went down to the laboratory with a definite question in mind about "how you can send telegrams under water," and he and Tom sent messages to each other under water with great success and enthusiasm. This led to the plan of setting up a telegraph system between our class room and the laboratory. Jane,

Margery, Jason and Walter worked on this and
got it into working order.   They proceeded to
invent a code for their messages, but the technique of using this proved too much for them and
the sending of messages back and forward was
so disturbing to the rest of the group that, on
Miss Pratt's advice, the telegraph was taken
down, and experimentation in sending messages
for the present, confined to the laboratory.

ORIGINAL STORIES

"Big Hide, the Cowboy"—Dictated

Oh, look at the cowboys on the plains, herding
up the cattle, throwing the lassos and catching
and branding the steers! Big Hide, the cowboy,
is riding his broncho—the broncho is jumping,
swerving, Bucking![2] Big Hide can't be thrown,
he holds on tight with his knees, his spurs are digging into the flanks of the horses. Pink Nose, the
horse, is kicking fiercely. The black steer has
been thrown by Black Hide, the branding iron is
sizzling on the hair and making the number of the
ranch, 24 V.H. Now the cattle are near the river,

[2] Bucking is spelt with a capital at Jason's request, "to
make it wild."

they are plunging in like a mass of foam. The cowboys have lost control of the cattle, they are whooping and shouting, they are trying hard to herd them up again. Big Hide has thrown the bull! The rest are goring and horning each other because they want to get to their leader. The other cows have trampled their leader. Now the cowboys are chasing the herd further and further east. Now they have got them in the corral and are quieting them down and ready to sleep. The cowboys' work is now over, they are trailing home with sweating horses.—By Jason, Harry and Walter.

"Western Life"—From Original Manuscript

Big Bill—Chapter

The cowboys are rounding up two thousand steers and cows. Just then we heard the rumbling of thunder. When the bulls heard the thunder, they began to plunge and rear and we had a terrible time trying to drive them toward the shed. We got all of the cows and calves in the shed. Then we had to fire pistols to make the bulls move toward their shed. Then we got two of the fiercest bulls corralled; then the other younger bulls got quieted down and didn't have very much trouble getting them in their shed. The next day we let the cattle out to graze while we got ready for a buffalo hunt; all the cowboys got their guns and pistols and then we started off. We sent some other cowboys ahead to see if they could see any buffalo. Then one of the cowboys came galloping back and said they had seen a big herd of buffalo and one of the cowboys had seen a band of savage Indian warriors which were coming fast. Then all the cowboys prepared for a battle. They drew their pistols from the sheathes and loaded. Then they galloped away as fast as the wind.

CHAPTER II

Suddenly a savage Indian warrior rode up in front of me. He was fine to look at his face was painted with crimson with designs of hatchets, bows and arrows. He took his bow from his shoulder and drew an arrow from his quiver, then took careful aim and fired. The Indian fell from his horse dead. Then I saw four Indians appear. They took aim at one of the cowpunch-ers. He let the arrow fly, but the cowpuncher jumped from his horse. The arrow whizzed over his head.

"The Story of Fluffy Tail"

By Herbert Fuller

I was born in a cold rocky den. My father was the leader of one hundred savage wolves. And he wanted me to be a savage wolf like him. One day he took me out hunting for some deer while we were following some elk tracks we suddenly heard the thud-thud-thud and a cowboy rode up. Then my father snarled and the hair on his back stood up on end with rage. Then he got back on his haunches ready to spring but the cowboy was too quick for him.

EDUCATIONAL TESTS

In May, a Thorndyke-McCall reading test was given to the whole group of eight years old children, with the following results, expressed in terms of "reading age":

Alice	13 years	2 months
Walter	11 years	9 months
Emma	11 years	3 months
Vera	10 years	10 months
Leonard	10 years	10 months
Nell	10 years	4 months

Bertha	10 years	4 months
Grace	9 years	8 months
Jane	9 years	2 months
Elizabeth	8 years	8 months
Harry	8 years	1 month
Jason	7 years	9 months
Margery	7 years	0 months

Of these children only Harry, Emma and Alice had read before entering Group VII, so this represents for all the rest two years of reading. Harry did not at all do himself justice, as he was so slow getting to work that time was up before he had finished half his paper. All the answers he had time for were accurate and he is really able to read any stories he likes.

Margery and Jason have had special coaching by a student teacher in quick reading from flash cards to get them sufficiently launched before the end of school to read for pleasure during the summer. I have also given them special work in spelling from dictation, choosing chiefly phonetically spelt words and this proved so popular that other children have joined voluntarily. There is no one in the group even including these two poor readers who does not read for pleasure and demand time for it on the program, but Jason needs a specific type of content, Indians or primitive man, with much action to hold his interest.

NUMBERS

A standardized number test given to the group showed every one to be up to grade (3A), four to be one grade, two, two grades, and one child three grades ahead. The showing would have been much better, had not the group fallen into the bad practice of pointing off every answer with two decimal points, although the actual subtraction, addition, etc., was accurate. This was due to their store work and constant dealing with dollars and cents.

BOOKS READ BY CHILDREN IN APRIL

(*Whole book not read.)

Randall read: "Boyhood of Buffalo Bill," "Book of Cowboys."*

Herbert read: "Children of the Cliff," Dopp's "Early Plainsmen," Baldwin's "Explorers of the Northwest."*

Alice read: "Lolami, the Cliff Dweller," Bailey's "Flint," "Book of Knowledge,"* "The Indian Story Book" (Wilson).

Jane read: "My Book House."*

Grace: "Just So Stories,"* "My Book House."*

Vera: "My Book House."

Margery: "Just So Stories,"* "The Book of Knight and Barbara."

Harry: "Dokos, the Little Indian Boy," "Privateers of '76" (Paine), "Play Awhile Reader."

Bertha: "Colonial Stories" (Tappan), "Poems of Childhood" (Field).

Elise: "Donkey John" (Morley).

Leonard: "Mewanee," "Children of the Cliff," "Lodren, the Lake Dweller," "Apauk."

Jason: "Mewanee,"* "Children of the Cliff."

Emma: "Colonial Stories," "Explorers of the Northwest."

Elizabeth: "Little Dog Ready."

Nell: "Moni, the Goat Boy" (Spyri), "Donkey John."

BOOKS READ TO CHILDREN BY TEACHER

(*Means read aloud to group.)

"Story of a Piece of Coal," Martin.

"Commercial Geography," Robinson.

"Story of the First Pencil," L. S. Mitchell.*

"Pencil Geographic Leaflets," published by Dixon Co.

"How the World Is Clothed" (rubber), Chamberlain.*

"Geography and Industrial Studies," Allen.

"The Jungle Book," Kipling.

"A Visit to a Coal Mine," Cooke's "The World at Work."

XI

A CHILD'S WORLD

I

In few places has the belief been so amply justified that children are innately creative as in the Walden School. Few places perhaps have had the same conviction that given an environment which is creative and dynamic, that children will develop creatively and dynamically. Too many institutions write "Freedom" and "Self-Expression" large in prospectus and platform, but continue old methods of repression and routine in their classrooms. But the Walden School has actually managed to get and to keep the child's view of the world, and has built itself around that view. It really is, as its founder Margaret Naum berg first called it, the Children's School.

A world to be real to a child, says Margaret Pollitzer, must be child size. In it must be materials he can handle and use, avenues he can explore. He must be able to give body to his fancies in paint or clay or block form, or act them out with others who share his interests. Bernard

Shaw once declared that schools are prisons where the immature are confined a given number of hours a day to keep from bothering the mature. They are indeed prisons in more ways than one. Not only do they imprison the child physically, keep him cramped and silent all day in a single desk or room, but they imprison his mind and spirit as well.

With the results we are all sufficiently familiar. But the Walden School has dared to create a child's world and then for the most part to stand aside and watch the children grow in it under conditions of real freedom. This applies not merely to the daily round of activities, but to the treatment accorded each individual as well. A child may have all possible outward freedom, but still be hampered by personal inhibitions and subjective difficulties. These difficulties must be intelligently handled before the child can really function to the full extent of his powers. As will be brought out later, there is undoubtedly a connection between this subjective understanding of the children in the Walden School and the extraordinary results they attain in creative work of all kinds.

Unlike Miss Pratt's school there is no attempt to define activities at given age levels, although of necessity older children demand more formal instruction. Groups, according to Miss Pollitzer, are no more alike than the individuals composing them. A class of six-year-olds may be interested in studying boats one year and may embark upon an intensive study of waterways or of transportation. The following year the sixes may, because of summer-camp experience, become interested in primitive life and organization. "The school," says she, "is the child's world and the course of study evolves out of the problems and interests arising from the immediate community life, leading to further and further realms of study." This apparently hit-or-miss method of attacking subject matter does not leave the gaps in knowledge which one might expect. The children uniformly measure up extremely well in all the standard achievement tests and have a store of information frequently far in advance of their years. Some of the courses initiated by them are immensely interesting. During 1924 and 1925, for example, the twelve years old group studied anthropology with the help of Dr. A. A. Goldenweiser of the New School for Social Research. The course developed from an initial visit to wholesale markets and observation of the immigrant peoples in them. This led to a discussion of races and their cultures and various experts were invited by the children to address them on these subjects. Dr. Goldenweiser's material on the Iroquois Indians so interested them that they asked him to return and the course thus gradually developed. The stenographic notes of the sessions show an amazing intellectual acumen and range of knowledge on the part of the students. They discussed such topics as primitive cultures, taboos, superstition, religion, morality, inheritance of acquired characteristics, and toward the end of the first term outlined a text on anthropology for children, since no satisfactory one exists.

Similarly in science the children blaze their own trails and follow their own inquiries. A visitor tells of entering the science laboratory and seeing a dozen children of seven and eight years of age, absorbed in their work. Two or three were melting glass tubing preparatory to making thermometers, another group was experimenting with a steam engine, another with an electric battery, an eager pair were making ink. The children worked steadily, consulting one another in low tones, occasionally raised in the excitement of new discovery. Off in a corner the visitor discovered an adult, his back turned to the room, busily engaged in writing in a notebook. He paid no attention to the class, and the class paid no attention to him. Nobody had noticed the visitor's entrance. She was wondering a little what she ought to do, when a lad ran up to the man in the corner: "Oh, Slavie," he asked, *"what* is the heaviest thing in the world?"

"Slavie" regarded the boy thoughtfully for a moment, then drew a book from the shelf. "Here, look it up for yourself. I really can't remember."

The boy seized the book and looked at the title, "Whee-ee," he whistled, "that's chemistry!"

"Table of elements," suggested "Slavie." "Chapter eight or nine, I'm not sure which." He turned to the visitor.

"Are you the teacher then?" she inquired.

"Well, you can call me that," he replied, "at least I'm here."

But mainly he was there, he explained, as a convenience, only occasionally as a necessity. The materials and apparatus were within easy reach of the children. They could come and use them as they pleased. They could feel their way about, get acquainted gradually with Bunsen burners, test tubes, batteries, magnets, little engines, small dynamos, bells, carbons, voltmeters, lenses, rubber tubing, glass tubing, scales, charts, and reference books on science. A boy might begin in the spirit of play to heat glass tubing and find that it could readily be turned into various shapes. He might go from that to try to make thermometers, or as did one twelve years old boy to etching glass, a process that required weeks of research. In his class journal the boy published an account of his experiment, which he had carried on from beginning to end with no help whatever from his teacher.

ETCHING GLASS

"One time up at the science laboratory, I tried to etch glass, and after a few attempts I succeeded quite well. It was done in this way—

"I first melted some paraffin as smoothly as possible over a piece of clear glass. After it had hardened, I cut through the wax with a botany needle and made a small design and some lettering. I then poured some Hydrofluoric Acid (HF) over the wax, seeing that it covered the exposed glass, and then let it stand for about fifteen minutes. When I washed the acid off and scraped the glass clean from the wax, I found my design and lettering eaten into the glass.

"Hydrofluoric Acid must be kept in wax bottles because of its dissolving glass. The equation is as follows—

"$4HF + SiO_2 = SiF_4 + 2H_2O$."

A study of power houses and the uses of the dynamo and generator in the city's transportation

system grew out of the free play of the older
boys and girls with electrical apparatus. Excursions to factories, to electrical expositions, to a
power house of the subway, showed the children
how the principles they had discovered in the
school laboratory were applied to industry.

The children do not always come to the laboratory to "play." More often they come to seek
the answer to questions raised in the classroom,
or possibly in the domestic science kitchen. "Why
does water boil?" "Why does gas burn sometimes with a blue, and sometimes with a yellow
flame?" "Why does soap make dishwashing
easier?" [1]

The seven years old children had decided to
build a city in the back yard. They went to the
science laboratory to find out how to lay pipes,
how to make a concrete bed for their river, how
to equip the houses with an electric light system.
They discussed why oil had to be used on concrete. All knew that oil would prevent the concrete from sticking. "Why should it?" asked
"Slavie." A seven years old boy answered him.
"The wood has pores into which concrete goes
and sticks. But when you use oil, it fills up the
pores and prevents the concrete from sticking."

[1] See also "Creative Science Teaching," by R. S. Slavson,
School and Home, January, 1924.

The children discovered what proportions of sand, gravel and cement to use, and mixed their own concrete. In digging for the river bed they took up the study of rocks and learned the difference between granite, quartz, felspar and cinders. They even found some volcanic material in the fill of the soil.

Sketches were made of the tools and materials needed and some spelling drill was found necessary for the more difficult names: trowel, hoe, shovel, hammer, wedge, concrete, cement. After the city was built, histories were written of its making.

Such a method as the foregoing has little in common with that of the ordinary text book on science with its neat beginning of laws and principles and scientific terms to be learned by rote. But as Dewey long ago has told us, most teachers start where the expert has left off. In their haste to save the child's time and get him educated quickly, they assume that they can shortcut the process of experimentation and present the child with its finished conclusions. Under duress, the youngster may succeed in cramming down the indigestible lot of facts required, but of course he more rapidly succeeds in forgetting them when examination time is past. That loss is unimportant. What is important, however, is the lack of opportunity afforded the child for actual experimentation along lines related to his own interests, and of learning thereby the scientific approach to his own problems.

Such opportunities are abundantly offered in "Slavie's" laboratory. Moreover through the apparently haphazard experimentation of the early months, the children succeed later in solving problems in physics and chemistry frequently reserved for college grades. They also make things which few college students have the chance to make. Wet cells, plunge batteries, electric signs, resistance lamps, electrically propelled canal boats, moving picture machines, star finders are only a few of the products of children all twelve years old or younger.

Since children, if given the opportunity, will always prove creative, it is no more surprising that a child, given free play with science materials, should use these materials creatively and inventively, than that he should use color beautifully, dance, or model, or write with skill and a high degree of merit. The paintings of the Walden School children have been on exhibit for successive years at leading art galleries of the city and have attracted an unusual amount of attention from artists and professional critics who have been astonished at the originality, the design, the feeling for composition, the richness and color of the work.

Mrs. Cane, their gifted artist teacher, would probably disclaim all credit for these extraordinary results. Man, she believes, is born with the power to create. Almost any little child can learn to paint as naturally as to speak or to write.[2] They are all languages of his being, and their great value is as a channel of expression for the child's subjective life. If he be denied expression of his subjective life, he will be a starved and thwarted being.

With this faith in the child's natural creative power, Mrs. Cane employs none of the ordinary teaching methods. The children have no models, no instructions, few directions of any kind. They are given, from the earliest years, plenty of large paper, and crayons and paints. Mrs. Cane's directions are confined to simple technicalities concerning the care of their brushes, and paints, how many ways there are of retrieving work, by scraping with a palette knife, or using turpentine and a rag to wash it clean, or painting over obstinate parts with white paint. She never works on a child's canvas, and she never makes any suggestions of any kind unless she is asked to do so.

[2] "Teaching Children to Paint," by Florence Cane, *The Arts*, August, 1924, pp. 95-101.

Even then her suggestions seldom have anything to do with the canvas itself, but usually with the child's idea concerning the work. Usually there is some inner inhibition which prevents the child from going forward freely.

Fear of failure is the most usual inhibition. One little girl, she relates, had painted her first picture, a study of a jar of flowers, a rather conventional affair, and now she was sitting facing a blank canvas, desirous of doing something of her own creation, but fearing to make the plunge. "I can't paint!" she exclaimed after a little time had elapsed. "What would you paint," Mrs. Cane asked her, "if you could paint very well?" "An idea evidently came to her like a flash," Mrs. Cane writes, "for her face lit up and she began describing a scene that had recently impressed her. A gray sea and sky, a sandy beach, and a little old woman in black on the beach alone, looking out to sea. It must have made a strong impression on her, because the description came so clearly and with intense feeling. I said, 'Well, where would you put the edge of the beach?' Her hand made a quick line. 'And where would the sea and sky meet?' She drew another quick line. 'And the old woman?' I asked. She stopped and said, 'I can't draw an old woman with a shawl.' So I volunteered to pose. I drew a sweater over my head and shoulders like a shawl and turned my back. She sketched it roughly and thanked me. I left her and without further ado she finished the painting, and an extremely fine thing it was, full of the sense of the sea and grayness and loneliness. It was only her second painting, but the feeling she had about the scene carried her over the problems she met on the way. She forgot her fears."

It is because the children are working so freely and unconstrainedly, that their various forms of expression are so good a clue to their inner states of mind. In the ordinary school where the children are restricted and held up to an imposed standard, their products have a stereotyped uniformity that makes it almost impossible to distinguish one child's work from another's. But in the Walden School, each child's painting or writing is intrinsically his, and accurately represents his stage of development at the moment of its creation. The painting of one adolescent girl of a dimly drawn figure under the sea with a red tree of life on either side, could not have been done by any other child in the school, nor by the girl herself at any other period. Similarly the turbulent seas and wind strewn beaches drawn over and over again by a ten years old boy bore witness to his unhappiness over an unsatisfactory relationship with his mother. When through the efforts of the school psychologist and the boy's teacher, the mother became aware of the situation and changed her attitude, the boy's work immediately reflected his new confidence and serenity. He began to draw pastoral scenes, later turned to broad and powerful designs. The children are of course quite unaware of the symbolism of their work—the girl who pictured the gropings of her unfolding life, stated quite simply that she had drawn a picture of a girl under the sea—the picture sprang actually from her unconscious.

The teachers of the Walden School have learned to read the evidence afforded in the drawings, writings and other creative efforts of the children. If some of them perhaps carry this psychoanalytic interest—particularly in their vocabularies—to an extreme, it still remains true that the school is unusually perceptive of the subjective growth and needs of its children and unusually responsive to these needs.

In one sense neither Miss Pratt's nor the Walden School is experimental. These happy, vitalized children whom one observes in them are proof enough that what these schools are achieving is of supreme social worth. Bertrand Russell recently remarked that public schools have long demonstrated the possibility of giving instruction without education, that, in fact, any schoolmaster who was caught educating was quickly "given the sack." With the growth of schools like these, and with the gradual incorporation of their principles in the public-school system, it may come to pass that education and instruction will become identical—a thing never before achieved under the sun.

II

A few of the writings of the Walden School children are reproduced below (unedited as to spelling, punctuation or any other respect). None of the children of course have had formal "compositions" or formal instruction in grammar or spelling. Nor have they had any assigned themes, following the usual school procedure of enumerating the special points to be included. The children write when they have something to say, when some experience has touched off their will to that particular kind of expression. The experience may have been an excursion, a class discussion, some recent book or conversation. No one dictates the form, although frequently of course one child will start all the rest writing verse, or fairy tales or wild west stories.

No attempt was made to select the work of bril-

liant nor specially gifted children. The selections
were literally taken at random from the files. It
might therefore have been possible to find compositions possessing more literary promise. It
should also be added perhaps that the teachers of
the Walden School do not feel that the children
reach as high a standard in writing as in some of
the other means of expression. There is no member of the staff who is as sensitive to the art of
writing as Mrs. Cane, for example, is to painting.
The selections show sufficiently well however with
what freshness and charm children will write
when living in a free environment.

It has also seemed worth while to reproduce
at the end a few compositions of public school
children of approximately the same age, also
selected at random.

The Rain and I

It had begun to rain very softly and I wished
to go out. I did so watching the rain. I sat
down quietly thinking how lovely the rain was,
when a feeling came over me that made my heart
warm within me. My eyes closed and I could
hear the soft patter of the rain falling on the roof
and the deeper noise of the rain falling down into
the court. The feeling was still over me when
someone called me and instantly I lost this quiet
feeling and I became my louder self again.

LOUISE LEE (Age 11.11).

DAINTY RAIN

Soft light dainty rain
Dropping ever so softly on the World
Mingling with the sound of running water
Which is falling from the houses near by.

LOUISE LEE.

LITTLE CHILDREN

Little children dancing about in the rain
Opening their little hands to catch the playful
    drops
Oh, rain, Oh, rain, you pretty silver fairies
Play with us, play with us,
Wet our hair and we shall laugh,
Tumble us about in your fury
And we shall not mind.
Rain and rain forever
So we may play with you.

LOUISE LEE.

Lights — Lights — Lights — all colors, reds,
greens, yellows, glaring at you from all sides
looking like dragons and fearful monsters. But
they are all so crowded together, it is hard to
make out that they are advertisements of tires,
bottles of ginger ale, tooth brushes, chewing gum
and thousands of others.

Then you see the people rushing back and forth
in excitement, usually dressed in their best going
to theatres, dinners and a number of other places.

And they all blend into a mass of darkness and color.

ANNA FLEISHER (Age 12.9).

EVOLUTION

Nothing blue nothing green,
Everything a swirling whirling mass,
Crashing falling thundering,
Flames piercing through rock and gorge
A falling whizzing sound, a settling thud
All is quiet except for a hissing swishing
A heat that penitrates the most staunch barricades,
Then night—what is night
Darkness, blackness, silence.
A glow, a warm warm glow,
A sphere of red and yellow light,
Stars, moons, Planets,
Circling, swirving, twirling
Clouds passing,
Shape of animals, seas, spirals, vast mountains.
Now Water—wetness,
Cells, single cells lonely slowly rocking—floating,
They multiply, divide,
Swim side by side,
Crawling, sprawling, falling
Now plants, trees, vines that twine and climb
And after centuries and centuries of development
        Dinosaurs
Beasts whose hinds and fores could reach for
        miles and miles,
They swam and played and talked through genera-
        tions,

After eons of changing, these huge vertebrates
    were gone
Never more to return—extinct,
Out of this came Man.
            ANNA FLEISHER (Age 12.7).

I object to telling my thoughts about religion,
because they are very delicate. Like a soap
bubble. If I touch it, it bursts.
    I will say this though. I do not believe in any
established religion. And I do believe in something superior. But how I believe and feel about
it, is inside my soap bubble.
           ISABEL SOLOMON (Age 12.8).

We boast of having many things belonging to
us. How free we are. And the power of our
brains.
    Yet we belong to a world which may boast of
having all of us in its power. Try as we may we
cannot leave the earth, our master.
    We cannot overcome its powers with our best
products. It can send from its depths fire, water,
a mass of things and tear us to pieces. While we
scratch the surface with our dynamite, thinking
we are controlling the earth.
    We think we are strong, unconquerable. We
are not masters. There are other powers.
           JEAN WOLFSON (Age 13.1).

Darkness on all sides but one small hole. Low
jagged rock sticking out. Wet moist rock.
    A small dent in the rock, water has fallen here

for years. A small hole a foot in diameter inside a descent.

Low walls, a passage then a small opening. Water on top. Crystal clear flakes of snow. Below an ice floor. Another passage leading on. A wall.

Back again in the ice room, up the passage.

The hole—no, no hole at all. The horror of being cased in for ever. Dieing of want. Then the opening again.

Into the main cavern at the opening, and then light!

JEAN WOLFSON (Age 13.4).

A calm and beautiful stillness lay over me
I could not move
It was like a spider's web
So finely worked, so intricate,
I could not move
I was still and silent
I could not move.

ANNE WERTHEIM (Age 10.10).

A SNOW STORM

It covers the city like a mist
The wind blowing gaily about
Flurrying, hurrying it about,
Now I can see only the tops of the buildings,
But the snow is so flurrying
I almost see the buildings whirling
So flurrying is the snow.

ANNE WERTHEIM (Age 10.10).

I saw a great big snow flake gliding slowly down
to the ground.   On it I saw something which
looked like a girl and I think it was Diana.
                    KURT FETZ (Age 11.10).

The snow is made up of fairy like shapes,
Flittering around, wandering here and there.
Falling lightly, melting,
While some pile up and make a mountain of snow.
                    DIANA SIMON (Age 10.11).

AN INDIAN DANCE

With a sound that is hardly audible
The Indians start their dance.
The older man with rythm that is perfect,
They beat their tom tom on and on,
Slowly the beating stops
And the warrior take their places.
                    DIANA SIMON (Age 10.11).

WHAT THE CHILD OF 1825 THINKS

I heard a sound
I looked around,
I couldn't see a thing.
But now I know,
It's truly so!
It was the fairy king!

WHAT THE CHILD OF 1925 THINKS

Oh! something stirred!
I'm sure I heard

A movement of some kind!
Oh, ding bust gosh!
That's lots of bosh!
'Twas my subconscious mind!
                        WILMA SHORE (Age 11.3).

THE ADVENTURES OF BUSHY TAIL

Bushy Tail was a baby squirrel and a lively
squirrel. Why when he was about two weeks old
he was as lively as two squirrels about one year
put together. You know he could jump from one
tree to another as quick as a flash of lightning.
It was wonderful to see him jump, that is if you
could see him which you cant do unless you were
a squirrel too, because he was too quick for you.
The minute you came anywhere near him he
would scoot away into the farther recess of the
forest and there would start burying nuts, that
is if it was nut season. For you must know he
was a fox squirrel and he buried more nuts in a
year than a fox squirrel usualy does. He was
spry I'll say he was spry. He could beat a martin
in a straight away race in his home range and in
a regular race, that is a crooked race dodging and
hiding behind the trees in an unknown place. But
it sure was as hard as anything, that's what Bushy
Tail said and you can't blame him either. Because a martin can go through trees very quickly,
a squirrel can too but he usually gets caught.
Bushy Tail never did he always got away. It was
often luck I must admit. Because something else
would fortuneately lead the martin away from

him. And sometimes he would get away by using all the strength and speed that he had and could use. Well he was a thoroughbred squirrel no denying that. The only trouble with him he was too brave, too bold; he was too sure of himself. Why after he had a tricked a martin into killing himself he boasted altogether too much. But aside from that he was perfect.

Of course he wasn't the most marvelous squirrel in the woods but just the same he was very lively and full of fun and mischief, don't forget the mischief. But you know how it is nobody can be perfect, they can be almost perfect but not quite. Well he would frisk around with some other squirrels for about a day or two and then he would frisk away to find some other playmate either a squirrel or a chipmunk. That was another of his faults which I forgot to mention that was all. One day in the spring Bushy Tail disappeared the mating time had come. There was nothing strange about that. Only there was something strange about the fighting done in the forest in the last few days. All of a sudden the fighting stopped it was because Bushy Tail had mated and then he foolishly got caught by a boy who was coming along through the forest and spied and caught him before he could get away. That was careless of him alright then he got away in one day and was never carless again.

THE END

CHARLES ORDMAN (Age 9.6).

A Story of the War of 1812 and Other
Stories by M. Most [1]

Note-to-reader

I want you to get acquainted with this book
before you read the stories, so that you should
not misunderstand it.   First of all I want you to
know that this book is not a book of war stories
just because of the first story being a war story,
in this book there are different types of stories,
such as (war stories, fairy-tales, ghost stories and
animal stories etc. etc.) which are seldom found
in other books.   The reason why I did this was
because I had a lot of diffrent kind of ideas (for
stories) that could only fit in one book, so I wrote
them all down in one book and that was the
simplest thing that I could have possibly done.

M. Most.

P.S.   There are also poems in this book.

[1] Age: 10.5.

A STORY OF THE WAR OF 1812

Chapter I

Captain Lilienthal[2] (of troop A in the regiment No. 57 of the American Army) was called in to one of the higher officers of the regiment and was told that he had to go on the battle field against the Canadians. This was exciting news (although he had been expecting it for almost three months) so at once the preparations began. Now I have forgotten to tell you that this was one of the smallest of the troops in the regiment. This troop was composed of only 30 men (and this was some of their names;

Mr. Lilienthal (The Captain)
Mr. Most and Mr. Goldstein (The Two Spies)
Mr. Ordman (The Sentinel)
Mr. Spear and Mr. Glaser (The Guards)
Dr. Schwartze (The Doctor)
Miss Bare (The nurse)
Etc. Etc. . . .

and evry one of them was so excited that they could hardly stand on their legs. And so everything was prepared for the battle!

The end of chapter one

(Illustration here, entitled, "They begin their journey."—Ed.)

Chapter II

And then they travelled till night came. And then came their first hardship, for they soon found out that they were short of one cot. If such a

[2] (Names of characters are all Mr. Most's classmates.)

thing would have happened any other time then one of the soldiers woud take his blankets and sleep on the groun, but since it had rained the night before and the ground was to damp to sleep on without getting sick. But soon their troubles were over, becaus Mr. Goldstein and Mr. Most volunteered to sleep on the same cot, and since then they were very close friends.

Nothing important enough to write down happened after that while they were traveling so we will have to be content to find the troop in the place where they wanted to be. . . . Now we must picture in our minds Captain Lilienthal sitting on his cot while one of the privates came rushing in, his face as pale as a ghost. "What is it" asked the captain in his calm way. "An enemy's plane was sighted" answered the private. "What of that?" asked the captain. "Well—it—it threw a bomb on us—which landed 200 yards away from camp" answered the private. "Bad luck—send for the two spies at once," said Captain Lilienthal. And in a moment Mr. Most and Mr. Goldstein were hurrying away from camp.

The End of Chapter Two

(Illustration here, entitled "The Throwing of the Bomb."—Ed.)

Chapter III

After Mr. Most and Mr. Goldstein had been trotting for a few minutes Mr. Most said to Mr. Goldstein, "Now we have to part"—"Don't you remember what the Captain said," said Mr. Most, "so we will have to say goodbye, for we may not be able to see each other again." "I know what you mean" said Mr. Goldstein sadly, "but I hope it doesn't happen" he said as he troted slowly away. Mr. Most spied wherever he was told to spy, but he came back without any news, but Mr. Goldstein had, what we can call, an adventure. It was like this. After Mr. Goldstein had been trotting a while, he came to the enemy's camp that he was told to spy on. So he hid in some bushes and waited for a half an hour and then he saw a scout hurry away from the Canadian camp, so he followed the scout for a quarter of a mile and then shot him through the head and then (after examining him a great deal) he found a note in his shoe. He was so excited that he almost opened the letter and read it himself but then he remembered that the Captain had told him that (if he got anything) he should deliver it into his hands without reading it. So he trotted away towards camp. Now it happened that while Mr. Goldstein was shooting the Canadian scout, another scout happened to be near and heard the noise, so he followed Mr. Goldstein a little ways and then hit him on the head with a club and Mr. Goldstein fell immediately unconscious. And after that he couldn't tell what happened for what seemed to be an age. But any ways when he recovered his consciousness he found himself lieing in some hay in a tent that was so closed up that two germs couldn't squeeze through the biggest crack in the tent if they wanted to. He was tied to the ground by some ropes that were attached to some stakes which was hammered in the ground.

The End of Chapter III

Chapter IV

This was not very pleasing to Mr. Goldstein because if he was tied up, it was impossible for him to escape, while otherwise it might have been. Well, if it was possible or if it wasn't possible, Mr. Goldstein decided to *ESCAPE* "And he did"! ! ! It was like this:—

Harold (wich we shall not call by his second name any more, since we are getting to know him so well), was just about to make an efort to get up, when in came Captain Gilooly of the troop of wich Harold had been spying. Now something told Harold that Captain Gilooly was very kind, so he made believe that he was suffering very badly, because of the way he had been tied up. Now Captain Gilooly, thinking that Harold was suffering, had pity on him and untied him. Then Capt. Gilooly went out and left two guards at the entrance of the tent wich was closed. And then Harold got up from the hay and stood up in a corner of the tent and (when Capt. Gilooly came back to see how his prisoner was getting along) he made believe he had no desire to go away, but when Capt. Gilooly went out of the tent, Harold began to look around in the tent and in anther corner he found a strong stick. Just as he was about to pick up the stick he heard a sound, it came from the left of the tent, it sounded as if

someone was walking on hay and yet it didn't!!!
"Yes no yes—," he almost said it all aloud. It
was to much for Harold, he would find out by
himself. So he took the stick and made a big
hole enough for his hand to go thru (in the direction in which he had heard the sound). Then he
stuck his arm thru the hole and all he felt was
hay, instantly an idea came into his head—a way
to *ESCAPE!!!* He set to work immediately, he
took the stick and began to dig. He dug till the
morning and finally made a hole big enough for
himself to squeeze through. Now on the other
side of the tent was a big haystack, so when
Harold crept through the hole, he naturally was
under the haystack. Then he started a terrible
racket, so all the soldiers of the camp rushed in
the tent, and while they were trying to find out
how he escaped he crept out from under the haystack and ran for his dear life. And by the time
the Canadian soldiers found the hole that Harold
made, Harold was entering the American camp.
Then Harold looked in his pocket and found the
same note that he had taken from the Canadian
spy, for the Canadians that had imprisoned him,
had not known that he had had it.

(Illustration here, entitled "The tent of
Harold's imprisonment, notice haystack on right."
—Ed.)

Chapter V

Immediately Harold brought the note to Captain Lilienthal, and the Captain read it aloud. It
said:—

Dear Captain Price;

I (Captain Gilooly of troop R of the Canadian regiment, No. 10) meen to make an atack on troop A of the regiment No. 57 of the American army, so kindly lend me some of the forces of your troop, so that my atack may be more powerful.

Your fellow officer,
CAPTAIN GILOOLY.

For a while, after Captain Lilienthal had read the letter, there was a long silence, then Captain Lilienthal said; where did you get that note? Then Harold told his story ending with—it's a thing that happens once in a thousand years, but it *happened!*

.　　.　　.　　.　　.

Afterwards Captain Lilienthal sent for 60 more men and because they were so well armed they won.   And all because of Harold.

The End of Chapter V

(Mr. Most's book of "Short Stories" also ends here.—Ed.)

PUBLIC SCHOOL COMPOSITIONS

Many public school children write better "compositions" than the following.   There are gifted teachers who succeed in getting excellent results, as many school publications show.   The compositions reproduced below are representative however of the sort of thing that children write when the task is imposed, the theme limited, and the premium placed on conformity. Nobody for example believes that any boy would spontaneously write such a letter as the following:

400 Pleasant Street,
North Adams,
January 9, 1925.

DEAR JOE:

When I grow up, I am going to try to be like Abraham Lincoln. I have just finished reading his life and I am delighted with it. He is a man for American boys to imitate, I think. Such a splendid example of perseverance, endeavor and noble self sacrifice. I shall probably not become the President of the United States, as he did, but if I can be as honest, studious, persevering and kind hearted as well, I will be sure to succeed in life and make many friends.

Just think how he began! Why, I have twice as many advantages. So I shall do my best and keep my eyes on model. Wish luck to your friend,

TOM CHRISTIAN (6A).

THE INAUGURATION OF CALVIN COOLIDGE

Our thirtieth president Calvin Coolidge took his oath as president of the United States at Washington, D. C. It was a gala day in Washington.

President Coolidge was inaugurated at about noontime. He took oath on a great platform which was built for that purpose. The ceremony was said by Chief Justice Taft. The bible was a little bible his grandmother gave him when he was five year of age. The bible was held by a close friend of the President. Charles G. Dawes was elected vice president just before President Coolidge took oath. Over 6000 people were standing on the streets and watched President Coolidge go to the Capitol. President Coolidge after the inauguration went back to work.

SARAH TOWNSEND (6A).

March 5, 1925.

ARBOR DAY

Arbor Day this year is on April twenty-fourth. We have had Arbor Day over thirty-five years. We first had Arbor Day in Nebraska. Arbor Day is for planting trees and flowers. The earth is nearly useless without them.

Arbor Day is celebrated in school by planting trees and flowers. It is celebrated the first Friday in May or one of the last days in April. Arbor Day is spreading into every country. We need these trees. These trees make the earth look beautiful. Some trees bear fruit and we eat the fruit. It teaches children to love trees and learn what the trees give us.

ANNA ANGELINO (6A).

April 24, 1925.

The following six compositions were all written by members of the same 6A class following a visit to a library. Almost every child of the forty odd members of the class wrote an identical report:

> 67 Van Ness Place,
> New York City,
> March 13, 1925.

DEAR ANNIE:

One day in last week my teacher Miss Dean took us to the Library. Miss Brown the Librarian read to us a story the name Dr. Dolittles. We enjoyed it very much. Than Miss Brown told us to go and read the books silently. The name of the book I read is What Katy Did. I enjoyed it very much.

Than I read another book named the Laughing Prince. I am sure if you would be there too you would enjoy yourself there too. I very sorry that you were not there too

> Your loving friend,
> ELLA POLESI.

> 152 Howe Ave.,
> New York City,
> March 13, 1925.

DEAR MOTHER:

One day last week, my teacher took us out to the Library. When we came into the library we set down on chairs and Miss Brown, the Librarian

read to us a story about Dr. Doliitle.   It is a
very nice story.   He was a peoples Doctor, so and
he loved pets al kinds his house was full of
Animals.   So nobody wanted to come to him.
So he became a Animal doctor.   After a horse
came to him and he saw the doctor wear spec-
tacles, so he said I want the same thing but green
glasses.

After she finished the story we went and picked
out the boocks we liked.   And read silently to our
selves.   Then we went home and we were carefull
by crossing the street.

Your loving daughter,
ROSE PITSKY.

27 Hill Street,
New York City.

DEAR MARY:
One day last week we went to Library.
When we reached there everything was ready for
our class.   Miss Brown, the Librarian read us a
story called Dr. Dolittle.   It was a very enjoyable
story.

After the story was over she Miss Brown said
we can look and read some books.   As I brought
my own book I read that.   I forgot to tell you
that Chee Chee in monkey language means ginger.
Finally we were allowed to go home.   And on our
way out we all thanked her.

Your loving friend,
EFFIE AARONSON.

348 Willow Street,
Brooklyn, N. Y.

DEAR ROSE:

One day last week my teacher took our class to the Library. Miss Brown, the Librarian read the book that is called Doctor Dolittle to us.

After that Miss Brown said that Chee Chee in monkey language meant Ginger. Then she let us read any kind of a book we liked. There were funny books and fairy tales. I am sure you would enjoy the books that were there.

Your friend,
MINNIE MERKLE.

798 K Street,
New York City,
March 13, 1925.

DEAR MOTHER:

When the time came to go to the Libary our whole class went. Mrs. Brown the Librarian told us about a story called Dr. Dolittle and it was very interesting because it was about animals. First his sister told him that he was getting poor because more animals came. So one day the cats meat man came and told him to give up the childrens doctor and be a animal doctor. After she was in the interesting part she stopped and told us to look around and read books.

While looking around for a good book I found Jack and the bean stalk. I read about it and it was like this that he went to the giants house and killed them and took the gold.

Your loving son,
LOUIS LEVI.

THE STAR SPANGLED BANNER

During the War of 1812 a man wrote The Star Spangled Banner. This man's name was Francis Scott Key. This man wishing to secure his friend went on board the ship but instead of securing his friend they made him a prisoner.

This man wrote this hymn on the back of an envelope. But by the stout defense of Fort McHenry they couldn't conquer us.

JACK GLASS (6A).

February 20, 1925.

THE STAR SPANGLED BANNER

The Star Spangled Banner was written by an American man held prisoner on a British War Ship. This man's name was Francis Scott Key.

The British were firing very rapidly and wanted to get the American flag down. They fired at first at Fort McHenry but the Americans drew them back. But at last the British surrendured and the Americans won the war. And the American flag went up, and now we are independent.

DAVID STARR (6A).

Feb. 29, 1925.

THE STAR SPANGLED BANNER

While the War of 1812 a man was taken a prisoner on the British fleet. Because he went to see his friend and, he was taken as a prisoner.

During the night he did not sleep but was out on the deck to see who would win. While he was watching he wrote on the back of an envelope a poem called the Star Spangled Banner written by Francis Scott Key.

He watched all night to see if the American flag was still there, that would mean that the American won, if the British flag was up that ment that the British won.

IDA BELL.

Feb. 20, 1924.

XII

A NEW EDUCATION FOR LABOR

A TEACHER recently prophesied that the next heresy hunt will be directed against the rapidly growing number of people who believe in "experimental" education. Some canny sleuth will discover that there is a direct connection between schools which set out deliberately to train children to think, and to develop creatively, and the radical movement. Not all progressive schools of course will be banned. There are some mildly progressive institutions, often supported by large foundations, which are trying to prepare children to take their places more adequately in society as at present constituted, or believe that teaching techniques should be improved. They will be considered safe enough. The dangerous centers are those directed by people who have a vision of a new social order, and who believe that the way to prepare for it is to bring up a generation of free thinking, self-directing young people whose spontaneity, originality and native curiosity have not been stifled nor confined within narrow grooves of conformity.

Some sleuth will be certain to reach these conclusions, because organized labor has done so recently and suddenly. We say recently, although so radical an experiment as the Modern School in Stelton, N. J., has been run for years with the help of individual workers and certain unions. But the school at Stelton has been an isolated entity—a Tolstoyan voice crying in the wilderness of conflicting economic doctrines. Visitors to the school have been astonished that children without formal or with no instruction should achieve such frequently fine results in painting, in mural decoration, in rug weaving, in clay and pottery, no less than in ordinary academic subjects, and the humbler crafts of printing, shoemaking and forge work. But that children thus permitted to develop naturally and· creatively should later have anything to contribute to a social re-ordering of the world, organized labor has not until now widely appreciated.

Within the past year, however, leading unions have four times demonstrated their recognition of the organic relation existing between this new educational philosophy and the evolution of a better social order. The New York State Federation of Labor issued its revised educational program listing some thirty-five specific recommendations for the improvement of the schools.

Many of these recommendations have long been urged by organized labor and in many places secured through its efforts: free text books, medical and dental inspection and treatment, enforcement of compulsory education, vocational training, free state scholarships, extension of kindergarten classes and the like. Two new planks were included in this latest program which indicate labor's increasing awareness of the part to be played by education in the necessary changing of social conditions. One plank was headed, War and Education, and ran as follows:

The organized labor movement, always in the forefront of service, whether in war or in peace, believes war to be the greatest menace to civilization. The next war with its death ray, its disease germs and deadly chemicals, may mean the destruction of civilization. Already munition makers and those who profit by war are preparing for another war by their policy of financial imperialism and the propaganda for preparedness that goes with it. The organized labor movement cannot sit idly by without resisting the machinations of these selfish materialists who betray their country's best interest for profit. We must meet their propaganda for war with efforts to preserve peace. We must appeal to the hearts and minds of America's Youth to war for justice—political, social and economic—and not to war against their fellow workers of other countries. In this struggle of preserving the peace of the world and civilization itself which hangs in the balance, the schools can render yeomen service.

To achieve the ends desired by all useful and socially minded citizens, we urge the reconstruction of our school curricula to help root out those narrow ambitions and ancient animosities that haunt and dominate Europe and to replace them with a desire for coöperation. Our textbooks in literature and the social and natural sciences must be re-written to eliminate the glorification of war and to substitute the facts about war; its cold-blooded butchery; its elimination of the biologically fit through disease, starvation, unemployment and death; its misery because of economic chaos and its debts which bear so heavily upon the workers for the benefit of the profiteers and munition makers and financiers. Instead of stressing the glories of war let us stress rather the heroes of peace personified by such men as Gompers, Wilson, McDonald, Edison and the like. Efforts toward peace like the Hague Conferences, the Washington Conference, limitation of armament, outlawry of war and world coöperation should receive due consideration. Only by striving continuously and coöperatively for peace can civilization be saved and the lot of mankind improved.—(Adopted by 1924 convention.)

The other plank, Schools of the Future, bears more directly upon "experimental" education:

The World War has led to a reëxamination of various institutions and the service being rendered by them. The organized labor movement regards education as the key to a better life. After a careful survey of our educational system it is of the opinion that the time has arrived for a thorough-going reconstruction of our educational aims, methods, equipment and curricula with a view of bringing them into harmony with present-day life and so that they may function effectively in the preparation for social living.

Our present educational system needs wholesome revision where it is characterized by a traditional and outworn curricula and methods, is artificially motivated, secures discipline essentially through coercion, imposes adult conceptions of life on changing childhood, or is deadening in its influence because of regimentalized school procedure and lifeless and useless subject matter largely unrelated to problems of child life. Moreover it is sometimes characterized by merciless "speeding up" to fulfill artificially established forms and it fails almost entirely to help pupils to live creatively and richly their normal lives.

Our teachers and workers are of the opinion that the schools of the future must be built on freedom and coöperation, must liberate and organize the capacities of children through opportunities carried on under a curriculum as rich, varied and as fluid as the life of the children and their ever changing environment, and that the ideal teachers should be coöperators who provide favorable conditions for self-development.

This plank bears the same impress as the proposal made by the Teachers' Union of New York City, which after an intensive study of the leading experimental schools in and near the metropolis, submitted to the local educational authorities a well worked out plan for establishing a similar experimental center within the public school system itself. The proposal being promptly rejected by the board of education on certain technical grounds, the Union is now sounding out the possibility of making necessary changes in the state education law.

Within the year also, two important conferences were held by leading educators and representatives of organized labor. One conference launched an experimental residential school primarily for workers' children under the direction of Mr. and Mrs. William M. Fincke, who donated to the enterprise their 177-acre farm, with its numerous buildings, equipment and fifty head of dairy cattle, at Manumit, Pawling, N. Y. An association of people from the labor and educational world was formed to direct the affairs of the school, with A. J. Muste of Brookwood as chairman of the executive board.

The actual running of the institution is in the hands of faculty and students who share alike in the work essential to the upkeep of school and

farm, as well as in the government of the school
community itself. The children range in age from
nine to fourteen, but older groups will be added
each year until college grade or its equivalent is
reached. Academic work, pursued this year under a modified Dalton plan, is confined to four
morning hours, six days a week, releasing the
students for other activities, no less educational,
of their community life. These include not only
the necessary chores, both indoors and out—cooking, dishwashing, and housecleaning, milking and
feeding the stock, chopping and hauling the wood,
etc., but plenty of recreational and social activities
as well. Wholesome social living Manumit considers its most valuable educational factor.

"The heart and marrow of a school like ours,"
writes a member of the faculty, "is the community life. Community life itself is our definition
of that freedom and responsibility in which every
educational democrat believes. The community
life of our school is the socialized incarnation of
our belief in industrial democracy. It is our act
of faith in the labor movement and in that good
life, that rich and noble life for all, which the
labor movement is going to bring in."

The other conference of labor representatives
and educators launched the junior Youth Movement in America, a movement closely correspond-

ing to the organizations among children which have proved so successful on the continent. Pioneer Youth which operates under the auspices of the National Association of Child Development,[1] purposes to use constructively the leisure time of boys and girls from seven to eighteen. Through clubs and summer camps, conducted in the spirit of modern education, it is hoped "to encourage activities which will stimulate the critical and creative faculties of children, will liberate their minds from dogma and fear and will help each one to become a force for the reconstruction of society. . . . We believe that the salvation of society will require the elimination of the destructive military spirit, of race and national hatreds and of the exploitation of one man by another."

There is however no dogmatic teaching of these ideas on the part of the leaders of Pioneer Youth. It is no part of their aim to impose "isms" upon children, nor to attempt to turn out ready-made little socialists or radicals. Propaganda, they realize, has no place in an enlightened scheme of education: what is needed are opportunities for children to become free creative personalities.

[1] This name has recently been dropped and the organization operates under the name of "Pioneer Youth."

Accordingly in the camp run last summer for 148 boys and girls on the Fincke farm at Pawling, and in the nineteen clubs organized last winter in and near New York City, efforts were made to have the children engage in the ordinary, normal healthful activities that children love to engage in anywhere. Sports, hikes, farm work, swimming, nature study, dramatics, pottery, camp fire amusements, the publication of a camp journal, written, printed and illustrated with cuts by the children themselves—these filled the summer days. The management of the camp was put in the hands of the children, who elected their own chairman—a capable lad of twelve—decided on their daily program, and made and enforced rules of camp behavior. On occasion, social and economic problems were discussed.

"One of the finest things I ever learned," wrote the youthful editor of the camp paper, "came about from a discussion around the camp fire. The subject was about the reason for race prejudice. Up to that time I had never been prejudiced towards Negroes, Russians, Italians and Swedes, etc., but I had always maintained a severe attitude towards the Japs. At the beginning of the discussion I fervidly championed the recent Japanese Exclusion Act. A few sensible remarks against exclusion brought me back to my senses.

. . . I found then that my real reason in favor of exclusion was that I did not know the Chinese and Japanese as well as the other races. . . . The whole discussion started because of race prejudice toward colored people, which was proven to be wrong. In conclusion let it be said that many of the troubles of the world have been due to hatreds between mankind."

During the winter, several of the clubs undertook special investigations of social conditions. One is investigating fire traps in Harlem. Another is raising money and clothes for the West Virginia miners and is planning to visit textile, steel and mining centers. Other clubs are pursuing the ordinary activities of any young people's organization, except that the management of the clubs is democratic, military discipline and military ideals do not prevail, and efforts are made by the club leaders to develop each child's special capacities so far as possible.

By January, it had become apparent to alert labor unions that Pioneer Youth might become immensely important to the labor movement. On one of the coldest nights of the year, delegates from 103 unions attended a conference of Pioneer Youth to give it their support. Credentials were read and accepted from nine international unions, sixteen central bodies and seventy-eight local unions. These included the American Federation of Teachers, the International Association of Machinists, the International Brotherhood of Firemen and Oilers, the International Fur Workers, the International Brotherhood of Pulp, Sulphite and Paper Mill Workers, the International Ladies' Garment Workers, the International Pocket Book Workers, the Subway and Tunnel Constructors International Union, and the United Cloth Hat, Cap and Millinery Workers Union.

Union funds have kept the movement going: $500 from the International Ladies' Garment Workers, $400 from the International Fur Workers, and $300 from the New York District Council, No. 9 of the International Brotherhood of Painters, Paperhangers and Decorators. The conference passed a resolution calling on unions to raise a fund of $5,000. It was also reported that two camps will be run this summer, and the work extended to Pennsylvania and New Jersey.

Yet actually the number of children involved so far in Pioneer Youth is small—not more than two or three hundred. Why then does every kind of organization of laboring men hasten to endorse it? Is it merely due to the energy and zeal of Mr. Joshua Lieberman, secretary of Pioneer Youth, that all sorts of workers—plasterers, hod carriers,

carpenters, painters, electrical workers, iron
workers, printers, railway carriers, clerks, express
handlers, firemen and oilers, machinists and garment workers, furriers, leather workers, cap makers, hatters, millinery workers, neckwear workers, subway constructors, bakery and confection-
ery workers, cigar makers, butchers, laundrymen,
stage employees, paper workers, bookkeepers, pattern makers and teachers—come forward collectively with unqualified support? With due credit
to the services of Mr. Lieberman, we believe that
such widespread endorsement of an educational
project would scarcely be given by organized labor,
were labor not becoming increasingly aware of
the necessity of fundamental educational reform.

A century ago American labor helped to establish for the first time in any country the great
experiment of free and universal education. Successful as the experiment has been in many respects, signs are not wanting that the shortcomings of the present educational system are many
and serious, that indeed unless a more vital, and
dynamic type of education replaces the one now
prevailing, the public school will prove a stumbling
block to social and industrial progress. That
labor is once more taking an aggressive attitude
towards elementary education is one of the most
hopeful signs of the times.

XIII

FUTURE PUBLIC SCHOOLS

FOR many years the term "social" has been one to conjure with in education. The big impelling motive in education, we are told, is the social motive. "All our schools," says one superintendent, "elementary, intermediate, secondary and collegiate, must in the future strive to realize more fully the seven great social aims of education.[1] This number was enunciated by the National Education Association and included health, mastery of the tools of learning, good citizenship, worthy home membership, vocational effectiveness, wise use of leisure, and ethical character.[2] These were to be given to the child, not as good things in themselves, but because they develop in him capacities and abilities the better to discharge his social obligations. So widespread is this attitude towards education that already a number of scales have been devised to measure and test the results of instruction in these social outcomes. There are tests to measure civic habits,[3] others to de-

[1] "The Platoon School," by Charles L. Spain, The Macmillan Co., 1924.
[2] Bulletin No. 35, 1918, U. S. Bureau of Education.
[3] Chassell-Upton Citizenship Scale, Teachers College, Columbia University.

termine vocational fitness,[4] and even a general scale to measure individual and social behavior resulting from school instruction in such matters as health and accident prevention and other social attitudes and practices.[5]

This emphasis upon the social significance of the school's task followed naturally upon the sternly individualistic attitude towards education which marked our earlier schools. "Gradually there has come the conviction that the perpetuity of our democratic society depends upon a consciously developed means of carrying on our affairs as a group, in short upon a process of socialization in the schools. If we are to become efficient citizens in a society in which the individual determines the policies of government, we must acquire knowledge socially valuable, gain insight and interest in our common problems, be practiced in thinking and solving these problems . . . We must learn to *live* together before we as individuals can gain fullness of life through formal education." [6]

Important as this attitude is, it has in the past

[4] Thurstone Vocational Guidance Tests, World Book Co., Yonkers, N. Y.
[5] "A Scale for Measuring Individual and Social Behavior," Public School Publishing Co., Bloomington, Ill.
[6] "Development of Method," by William A. Maddox, chapter in "Twenty-Five Years of American Education," edited by I. L. Kandel, The Macmillan Co., 1924.

been conceived far too narrowly. It has implied a ready made fairly static adult scheme of living for which children by proper doses of "social instruction" might reasonably be prepared to play an efficient rôle. Such changes as might take place in this ordered society were all in the line of predictable progress, a progress expressed primarily in economic terms; more wealth, more mechanical invention, resulting in more widely diffused literacy and culture, and extension of our assumed enlightened civilization to the dark places of the earth.

Recently, however, and especially since the war, the old faith in automatic progress has been shaken. We hear more and more talk of the mechanical side of civilization outrunning the personal capacities of those who are to work that civilization. We hear frequent expression of fear that the time may come when we shall have our immense complicated machinery of economic life with none at hand to work it. This forces our attention away from the problem of adapting the child to the static or so called progressing world about him, and raises the problem how to make a developing prime mover in progress out of the child himself. Dynamic, free and creative personalities will be necessary if the vast social structure we are erecting is not to overwhelm us with its own weight. Such personalities are little likely to be produced by the older disciplinary school, or its modern counterpart, "the socially regimenting" school. The immense popularity of the conception of the "Robot" shows how sound instinct of the mass places discipline of and for itself at a discount. The great contribution of such educational experiments as we have been discussing is that each to a greater or lesser extent aims to free the child from imposed tyrannies, whether of subject matter or routine, and to permit him full play for personal development. The Dalton and Winnetka plans seek to free him from the necessity of observing identical progress with forty or forty-five other children of varying ability, and of following closely a daily allotted task. The wise use of intelligence tests also works for the freeing of the individual by calling attention to his differences and the necessity of adapting the course of study to his special needs. The work-study-play schools, through the systematic use of variety, seek to free the child from the close discipline of the single classroom, and to give him opportunity to test his powers at first hand in laboratory, playground and workshop. The Lincoln School provides not only variety of program, but through scientific research is clearing the curriculum of the dead weight of unusable subject matter and

content. Professor Collings advances still
another step; he boldly abandons the course of
study, and directs his efforts to helping children
do better the normal and wholesome activities
they naturally engage in anywhere. Such avow-
edly free centers as the classes maintained by Miss
Goodlander and Miss Irwin, the City and Country and the Walden Schools, break through not
only the traditional barriers of curriculum and
program, but provide a new set up on the child's
own level of interest and understanding, rich in
materials and opportunities for creative growth.
In many of these experiments also, some attempt
is made to apply the findings of modern psychological research, which recognizes not only the
profound differences in children's mental capacities, but also the necessity of freeing them emotionally, no less than physically, of all handicaps
to complete functioning.

While many of these freer principles are being
taught in teacher training schools, and are here
and there reflected in isolated classrooms, it is
unlikely that we shall see their very rapid extension in the public schools. We shall first have
to multiply very greatly the number of these experiments and gain for them wider public knowledge and support. The obstacles against their
general adoption seem indeed insurmountable.

We have to deal not only with the dead weight of inertia and tradition in the schools themselves, complicated in too many places by the tug and warfare of opposing political interests, but we have to reckon with a public that has no very great measure of faith in what schools anywhere are trying to achieve. There is still a strong popular notion that education, so called, is only "skin deep," that the real lessons of life are learned not from schoolmasters and books, but in the realities of the world outside. The school exists primarily as a necessary disciplinary agent, divorced alike from the interests and needs of the child, and of the community it was designed to serve.

The very appearance of the conventional schoolhouse testifies to the popular conception of its function. Those vast barrack like structures that fill our city streets, impersonally numbered P.S. 39 or 192, what are they but the visible embodiment of the disciplinary trend, differing ever so slightly in outward appearance from the armories of the military, or even the prisons. Into these sterile masses of masonry we send the little child, straight from the intimate and easy associations of home and neighborhood living. He walks through the great iron gates, through the long stone court, through the heavy wooden door, down long corridors, past countless rooms.

With him go a throng of other children, also of tender age. He and they are sorted out and placed in their little grooves in classroom 100, or 203. In place of the vivid chatter of home, silence is enjoined, in place of eager activity, passive sitting, in place of the natural give and take between himself and a comprehensible mother or father, he must yield obeisance to the teacher, and beyond her to the principal, and beyond the principal, to a still higher official, and so on through a whole superstructure of authority, all there to impose on him behavior that is strange, and tasks that have no meaning.

Small wonder that we have such absurd antitheses as school and society, or child and community, when school and child and society are thus made mutually exclusive. The best of our educational experiments return to earlier and more simple ways. The little boy in Miss Goodlander's class who exclaimed, "I like this school, because I know all about it and everybody in it," voiced a need of childhood of very deep significance. In our haste to provide "learning" on a wholesale scale for the mass of children, we have overlooked the very elements that make learning possible. Somehow or other we shall have to make school intelligible to the child, somehow make it merely another "home" where he may continue the happy business of living and learning through living.

This means, perhaps, that we shall have to modify considerably our ambitious school building schemes, the erecting all over the land of mammoth and magnificent mausoleums, with their finished equipment and standardized facilities. A wise friend recently remarked that rather than subject young children to the inhibitions of monumental masonry and overwhelming systems, it would be far better if "school" for the youngest ones especially were merely a pleasant room or two over a millinery shop. By this he did not mean that the child should be given fewer, but rather more opportunities on a plane that he can understand, that he can manipulate and manage.

To be sure such complete changes as we urge would not be cheaply acquired. We should have to exceed our present bare 2% of our national income now spent on schools. We might have to approach the 10% which all budget experts agree should be spent on education. (What private individual educating his children in private schools would be content with spending so small a proportion?) To make such sums available, we might have to hasten long needed changes in our taxing systems. We should also have to face the ire of the economists, or rather the economizers—

(Pritchett and Co.). Our educational expenditures have indeed risen, although the increase has not been as rapid as that of other governmental activities, such as charities and corrections, or health and sanitation. Indeed a much smaller proportion of the tax dollar than formerly, is spent on education. Moreover while the school population has grown more rapidly than the total population, while modern communities demand additional and more costly facilities, especially for their high schools, the real cause of mounting educational costs is the decreased purchasing power of the dollar. School expenditures for such years as 1918 or 1920, when corrected to conform to the purchasing power of money in 1913, show an actual decrease.[7]

The popular notion dies hard that there is some unique relation between learning and discipline. Teachers who experiment with freer practices have to contend not only with the moss grown prejudices of other pedagogues, but with the shocked disapproval of the parents of their pupils. At least in the beginning they meet with such opposition. Later, as the newer practices bear fruit, parents may become the most active

[7] See summary of report of Educational Finance Inquiry conducted by American Council of Education, contained in chapter on the United States in Educational Year Book, 1924, The Macmillan Co.

protagonists of more modern ways. The parents of many children attending non-platoon schools in Detroit, have urged the extension of work-study-play schools to their districts; parents who in the early days of Miss Pratt's school withdrew their children because they did not immediately learn to read and write, are now moving down into the neighborhood of the school in large numbers.

The desire for fundamental education reform is evident both within school systems and without. Whole school systems, such as Winnetka and Gary are committed to the more liberalizing principles. The Dalton plan is making its way into many places formerly thought impervious to new doctrine. Although the actual number of "progressive" schools and radical experimental centers is still small, modifications in line with their teachings are gradually finding their way into many school systems. As such ideas gain wider acceptance we are likely to hear less about the difficulty of applying them under public school conditions. Overcrowded buildings and classrooms, undertrained teachers, meager equipment, and insufficient appropriations do seriously retard educational progress. Serious as such physical handicaps are, however, they are less an obstacle than the prevailing attitude towards education which

exists in the minds of those who run our schools.
Many of the experiments we have been discussing
are being tried out under public auspices. All of
them might be, and their number indefinitely increased, once the philosophy that underlies them
was held to be valid. Signs are not wanting that
this is actually taking place. There is a greater
questioning as to the aims of education and the
methods employed to realize these aims, informality in the classroom is no longer a complete anomaly, the center of interest is shifting
from the teacher and the course of study to the
child, and to him not as the enemy to be redeemed,
but as a creative personality, capable of indefinite
development. Taking the long look backward
enables Ex-President Eliot of Harvard to say,
"The progressive schools are increasing rapidly
in number and influence, and the educational public is becoming more and more awake to their
merits. They are to be the schools of the future
both in America and Europe."

APPENDIX

LIST OF EXPERIMENTAL AND PRO-
GRESSIVE SCHOOLS

(Supplied by Bureau of Educational Experiments,
144 West 13th Street, New York City) [1]

ANTIOCH COLLEGE AND ANTIOCH SCHOOL. Yellow
Springs, O.
Founded by Arthur E. Morgan of Dayton, O.
Co-educational, Kindergarten through College.
Literature available.

BEAVER COUNTRY DAY SCHOOL. Brookline, Mass.
Eugene Randolph Smith, Principal.
Co-educational, Kindergarten to College.
Prospectus.

BEAVER SCHOOL. 9 Beaver Place, Boston, Mass.
Margaretta Voorhees, Principal.
Co-educational Primary and Elementary
Grades. Prospectus.

BROOKSIDE SCHOOL. Upper Montclair, N. J. Anna
B. Gannett, Principal.
Founded by parents belonging to the Fairhope
League. No Prospectus.

---

[1] The Bureau in supplying this list stated that it is not
up to date, and asks that those having information of more
recent experiments write in about them.

BROOKWOOD WORKERS' COLLEGE. Katonah, N. Y.
A. J. Muste, Chairman.
Co-educational enterprise for the young people of the industrial class. Present enrollment 18 to 35 years of age.

CARSON COLLEGE. Flourtown, Pa. Elsa Ueland,
President.
Colony for orphan girls with special equipment
and educational advantages.
See, "What Keeps Children Well," by Marot
and Willets; also "Mother and Child," Aug.,
1922.

CHEVY CHASE COUNTRY DAY SCHOOL. Chevy
Chase, Md. Stanwood Cobb, Principal.
Primary to College Entrance.
Mr. Cobb was secretary and organizer of the
Progressive Education Association.

CHILDREN'S UNIVERSITY SCHOOL. 10 West 72nd
Street, N. Y. Miss Helen Parkhurst, Di-
rector.
Model School of the Child Education Foun-
dation. Montessori Class through High
School. No prospectus.
See, "The Dalton Laboratory Plan," by Eve-
lyn Dewey. E. P. Dutton, 1921.
"Education on the Dalton Plan," by Helen
Parkhurst. E. P. Dutton, 1922.

CITY AND COUNTRY SCHOOL. 165 West 12th
Street, N. Y. Caroline Pratt, Director.
Three Years to Thirteen Years.

Affiliated with The Bureau of Educational
Experiments.
See Bulletins Nos. 1, 3 and 8, Bureau of Edu-
cational Experiments.
Record of Group 6, City and Country School
Bulletin, 1922.
Experimental Practice in the City and Coun-
try School, by Caroline Pratt, with a Record
of Group VII, by Lulu Wright. E. P. Dut-
ton, 1924.

EDGEWOOD SCHOOL. Greenwich, Conn. Euphrosyne
Langley, Principal.
Kindergarten through High School.
Affiliated with the Fairhope League. Brief
prospectus available.

ETHICAL CULTURE SCHOOL. Central Park West
and 63rd Street, N. Y. C. Dr. Franklin C.
Lewis, Principal.
Branch School conducted by Mabel R. Good-
lander at 27 West 75th Street.
Literature available.

FAIRHOPE SUMMER SCHOOL. Greenwich, Conn.
Marietta L. Johnson, Director.
Summer normal course under the auspices
of the Fairhope Educational Foundation.
Classes of children for purposes of demonstration. The Edgewood school buildings
and grounds and the adjacent plant of Rose-
mary Hall School are used.

FAIRHOPE ORGANIC SCHOOL. Fairhope, Ala. Marietta L. Johnson, Director.

Kindergarten to College entrance.
Some resident students admitted.
See "Schools of To-morrow," by John Dewey,
Chap. II. E. P. Dutton, 1916.

FRANCIS SCOTT KEY SCHOOL. Locust Point, Baltimore, Md. Persis Miller, Principal.
A public school with special community service development.
Used as a laboratory for mental hygiene studies by Dr. Adolph Meyer, Johns Hopkins Department of Psychiatry.

FRANCIS W. PARKER SCHOOL. San Diego, Cal. Ethel Dummer Mintzer, Principal.
Open air school with special features of equipment. Prospectus available.

GARY SCHOOLS. Gary, Ind. Wm. E. Wirt, Supt.
"The Gary Schools," by Randolph Bourne. Houghton Mifflin Co.
"Schools of To-morrow," by John and Evelyn Dewey. E. P. Dutton, Chap. VII and IX.
"The Platoon School," by Chas. L. Spain. Macmillan, 1924.
Bibliography and bulletins may be secured from U. S. Bureau of Education. (Address Alice Barrows.)

JUNIOR ELEMENTARY SCHOOL. Downers Grove, Ill. Lucia B. Morse, Principal.
A laboratory school for little children, conducted by The Kindergarten Extension Association. Lucia B. Morse, Director.

LINCOLN SCHOOL OF TEACHERS COLLEGE. 425 West 123d Street, N. Y. C. Dr. Otis W. Caldwell, Director.

Experimental school of the General Education Board.

First Grade to College Entrance.

Descriptive Booklet and bulletins available.

PUBLIC SCHOOL No. 64. New York City.

Public school experiment under joint auspices of City Board of Education and Public Education Association. Aims to develop model Health and Mental Hygiene Service for city schools. Elisabeth Irwin, Acting Principal.

LOOMIS INSTITUTE. Windsor, Conn. Nathaniel Horton Batchelder, Headmaster.

High School age, prepares for business and college.

Endowed, located on a farm. Prospectus available.

MANUMIT SCHOOL. Pawling, N. Y. Henry R. Linville.

School primarily for workers' children, under control of Manumit Associates, a group of educators and labor representatives.

Printed matter available.

MERRILL-PALMER SCHOOL. Detroit, Mich. Edna White, Director.

Girls—High School and College age.

Endowed school for home-making arts and sciences. Conducts a nursery school for children 2 to 6 years. Mrs. Helen T. Woolley in charge.

THE MODERN SCHOOL. Stelton, N. J.
Boarding and day school conducted by the Ferrer colony at Stelton.
Children from four years of age. No Prospectus.

MORAINE PARK SCHOOL. Dayton, Ohio. Frank D. Slutz, Principal.
Founded by a parents' association under the leadership of Arthur E. Morgan. Interesting Prospectus and Year Book.

OAK LANE COUNTRY DAY SCHOOL. Philadelphia. Francis M. Froelicher, Headmaster.

OJAI VALLEY SCHOOL. Ojai, Calif. Edward Yeomans, Gudrun Thorne-Thomsen.

OLD ORCHARD SCHOOL. Leonia, N. J. Mrs. Anna G. Noyes, Principal.
A home school for limited number of little children.
Boarding and day pupils. Brief Prospectus.

THE PARK SCHOOL. Liberty Heights, Baltimore, Md. E. M. Sipple, Headmaster.
Founded and financied by a parents' organization.
Eugene Randolph Smith was the first principal.
Primary to College entrance. Prospectus available.

THE PARK SCHOOL. Jewett Avenue and Main Street, Buffalo, N. Y. Leslie Leland, Principal.

Kindergarten to College.
See, "A Peep Into the Educational Future,"
by Dorothy Canfield Fisher. *Outlook,* Sept.,
1915.
Prospectus available.

THE PARK SCHOOL. Cleveland, Ohio. Mary Hammett Lewis, Principal.
Organized by a group of parents. Mrs. Albert
D. Levy, Treas.,
Primary and Elementary Grades.

PETERBOROUGH SCHOOL. Peterborough, N. H.
Originally a vacation school for the children of
the Peterborough summer colony.
See "A School in Action," published by E. P.
Dutton Co.

PHOEBE ANNA THORNE SCHOOL. Bryn Mawr,
Penna. Frances Browne, Director.
Open-air school with special buildings and
equipment.
Used as a laboratory by the Bryn Mawr College Department of Education and of Psychology. Prospectus.

PORTER RURAL SCHOOL. Kirksville, Mo. Mrs.
Marie Turner Harvey, Principal.
See, "New Schools for Old," by Evelyn
Dewey. E. P. Dutton, 1918.
A rural school. First Grade to College Preparatory.

RAYMOND RIORDAN SCHOOL. Highland, Ulster Co.,
N. Y. Raymond Riordan, Principal.

An American adaption of the European "New School" idea.

Mr. Riordan was formerly instructor at Interlaken.

Woods and camp life featured.

Elementary and High School age. Prospectus available.

SCARBOROUGH SCHOOL. Scarborough-on-Hudson, N. Y. A. W. Sutherland, Principal.

Organized by a parents' association under the leadership of Mr. and Mrs. Frank A. Vanderlip. Prospectus available.

SILVER BAY SCHOOL. Silver Bay, N. Y. C. C. Michner, Pres.

Boys' boarding school, employing latest teaching methods.

High School age. Prospectus.

SUNSET HILL SCHOOL. 420 West 57th Street, Kansas City, Mo. Helen Ericson, Principal.

Kindergarten to College. Prospectus available.

THE UNIVERSITY ELEMENTARY SCHOOL. Columbia, Mo.

Laboratory school of the University's Department of Education.

See, "Child Life and the Curriculum," by Junius L. Merriam.

See, "Schools of To-morrow," by John and Evelyn Dewey, Chap. III.

UNQUOWA SCHOOL. Bridgeport, Conn. Carl Churchill, Principal.

Organized by a parents' association.

WALDEN SCHOOL (formerly The Children's School). 34 West 68th Street, N. Y. Margaret Pollitzer and Elizabeth Goldsmith, Directors. Margaret Naumburg, Educational Adviser.

Co-educational, 2 years through High School.

Founded by Margaret Naumburg. Prospectus and printed matter available.

WINNETKA SCHOOLS. Winnetka, Ill. Carleton W. Washburn, Supt.

School system developed around progressive ideas.

Printed matter available.

BIBLIOGRAPHY

Adams, John: "Modern Developments in Educational Practice." Harcourt, Brace and Co., 1922.

Baldwin, Bird T., and Stecher, Lorle: "The Psychology of the Pre-school Child." D. Appleton and Co., 1924.

Binet, A., and Simon T.: "The Development of Intelligence in Children." Baltimore, Williams and Wilkins, 1916.

Bobbit, F.: "The Curriculum." Houghton Mifflin, 1918. "What the Schools Teach and Might Teach." Cleveland Educ. Survey, 1915.

Bonser, F. G.: "The Elementary School Curriculum." Macmillan, 1920.

Bolton, F. E.: "Everyday Psychology for Teachers." Scribner's, 1923.

Bureau of Educational Experiments, New York: Bulletins: "Playthings," Revised, 1923. "Animal Families in School," L. B. Garrett. "The Play School." "The Children's School," Teachers College Playground, Gregory School. "Stony Ford School," The Home School. "A Catalogue of Play Equipment," comp. by J. L. Hunt, revised 1922. "Education Through Experience," Ethical Culture School, 1921. "School Records," by Mary S. Marot. "A Nursery School Experiment," by Harriet Johnson, revised 1924.

272

Burnham, W. H.: "The Normal Mind," D. Appleton & Co.

Bourne, Randolph: "The Gary Schools," Houghton Mifflin Co., 1916. "Education and Living," The Century Co., 1917.

Caldwell, Otis W. and Courtis, S.: "Then and Now in Education," World Book Co., 1924.

Chambers, Smith, and others: "Report of Experimental Work in School of Childhood," Univ. of Pittsburgh, 1916.

Charters, W. W.: "Curriculum Construction," Macmillan, 1923.

Children's Foundation: "The Child, His Nature and Needs," Valparaiso, Ind., 1924.

Coe, George A.: "Law and Freedom in the School," Chicago Univ. Press, 1924.

Cooke, H. C.: "The Play Way," Stokes.

Collings, Ellsworth: "An Experiment with a Project Curriculum," Macmillan, 1923.

Cubberly, E. P.: "Public Education in the United States," Houghton Mifflin, 1919. "The Principal and His School," Macmillan, 1923.

Dewey, John: "Educational Essays," London, Blackie and Sons, 1910. "How We Think," Heath, 1910. "Interest and Effort," Houghton Mifflin and Co., 1913. "School and Society," Univ. of Chicago Press, 1915. "Democracy and Education," Macmillan, 1916. "Schools of Tomorrow" (with Evelyn Dewey), E. P. Dutton, 1915. "Human Nature and Conduct," Holt, 1922.

Dewey, Evelyn: "The Dalton Plan," E. P. Dutton, 1922. "New Schools for Old," E. P. Dutton, 1920.

Freud, Sigmund: "A General Introduction to Psychoanalysis," Boni and Liveright, 1921.

Gesell, Arnold: "The Preschool Child," Houghton Mifflin, 1923. "The Mental Growth of the Preschool Child," Macmillan, 1924.

Green, Geo. H.: "Psychoanalysis in the Classroom," G. P. Putnam, 1921.

Gruenberg, Benjamin: "Outlines of Child Study," The Macmillan Co., 1923.

Hall, G. Stanley: "Aspects of Child Life," Ginn and Co., 1907. "Youth, Its Education, Regimen and Hygiene," D. Appleton & Co., 1909.

Hartman, Gertrude: "The Child and His School," E. P. Dutton, 1922. "Home and Community Life," E. P. Dutton, 1923.

Henderson, C. H.: "What Is It to be Educated?" Houghton Mifflin, 1914.

Hamaide, A.: "The Decroly Class," tr. by Jean Lee Hunt, E. P. Dutton, 1924.

Hill, Patty, Smith and others: "Experimental Studies in Kindergarten Education," Teachers' College publications. "A Conduct Curriculum," dir. by Patty Hill, and compiled by Burke, et al, Scribners, 1923.

Hinkle, Beatrice M.: "The Recreating of the Individual," Harcourt, Brace and Co., 1923.

Hollingsworth, Leta: "Special Talents and Defects," Macmillan, 1923.

Hunt, Johnson, Lincoln: "Health Education and the Nutrition Class," E. P. Dutton, 1921.

Horn, J. L.: "The American Elementary School," The Century Co., 1923.

Hosic and Clark: "Brief Guide to the Project Method," World Book Co., 1924.

Irwin, Elisabeth and Marks, Louis: "Fitting the School to the Child," Macmillan, 1924.

James, William: "Talks to Teachers on Psychology and to Students on Some of Life's Ideals," Henry Holt, 1916.

Johnson, Buford: "The Mental Growth of Children," E. P. Dutton, 1924.

Jennings, Meyer, Watson, Thomas: "Suggestions of Modern Science Concerning Education," Macmillan, 1917.

Judd. C. H.: "Evolution of a Democratic School System," Houghton Mifflin, 1918.

Kandel I. L.: Editor, "Twenty-five Years of American Education," Macmillan, 1924. Editor, "Educational Year Book," Internat. Institute of Teachers College, Macmillan, 1925.

Kilpatrick, W. H.: "The Project Method," series of papers, Teachers' College Record, 1918 and 1921, also "Jo. of Educ. Method," 1921. "The Montessori System Examined," Houghton Mifflin. "Froebel's Kindergarten Principles Critically Examined," Macmillan. "Source Book in Educational Philosophy," Macmillan, 1924. "Foundations of Method," Macmillan, 1925.

Lincoln School, Teachers College, New York: "Descriptive Booklet" and many pamphlets.

Long, Constance: "Psychology of Phantasy," Moffat, Yard and Co., 1921.

McCall, W. A.: "How to Measure in Education," Macmillan, 1922. "How to Experiment in Education," Macmillan, 1923.

McMillan, Margaret: "The Nursery School," E. P. Dutton, 1921. "Education Through the Imagination," D. Appleton, 1924.

McMurray, Frank: "A School in Action," E. P. Dutton, 1923.

Meriam, J. L.: "Child Life and the Curriculum," World Book Co., 1920.

Miller, H. C.: "The New Psychology and the Teacher," Thomas Seltzer, 1923.

Mirick, Geo.: "Progressive Education," Houghton Mifflin.

Monroe, DeVoss, Kelly: "Educational Tests and Measurements," Houghton Mifflin, 1917.

National Education Association: "Com. on Reorganization of Elementary Education," World Book Co.

National Society for the Study of Education: "Intelligence Tests and Their Uses," 21st Year Book, 1922. "Education of Gifted Children," 23d Year Book, Pub. School Publishing Co., 1924, Bloomington, Ill.

New Republic: Educational Supplement, "The Elementary School," Nov. 12, 1924.

New York Society for the Experimental Study of Education: "Contributions to Education," Vol. I, World Book Co., 1924.

Nifenecker, Eugene: "Pupil Progress Through the Grades," New York City Department of Education, 1922.

Norsworthy and Whitley: "Psychology of Childhood," Macmillan, 1918.

O'Shea, M. V.: "Mental Development and Education," Macmillan, 1922. "First Steps in Child Training," Valparaiso, L. E. Myers and Co., 1920. "Dynamic Factors in Education," Macmillan, 1909.

Parkhurst, Helen: "Education on the Dalton Plan," London, G. Bell and Sons, 1922.

Parker, Francis, School: Bulletins.

Pratt, Caroline E.: "Experimental Practice in the City and Country School," E. P. Dutton & Co., 1924.

Progressive Education: Quarterly of Progressive Education Association, Washington, D. C.

Robinson, J. H.: "Mind in the Making," Harper Bros., 1922. "The Humanizing of Knowledge," Doran, 1923.

Roman, F. W.: "The New Education in Europe," E. P. Dutton & Co., 1923.

Rugg, H. O.: "Statistical Methods Applied to Education," Houghton Mifflin, 1917.

Spain, C. L.: "The Platoon School," Macmillan, 1924.

Sies, A. C.: "Spontaneous and Supervised Play in Childhood," Macmillan, 1922.

Smith, E. R.: "Education Moves Ahead," Atlantic Monthly Press, 1924.

Stedman, Lulu M.: "Education of Gifted Children," World Book Co., 1924.

Stevenson, J. A.: "The Project Method," Macmillan.

Terman, L. M.: "Intelligence Tests and School Reorganization," World Book Co., 1922. "Suggestions for the Education and Training of Gifted Children," Stanford Univ., 1921. "The Measurement of Intelligence," Houghton Mifflin, 1916.

Thorndike, Edward L.: "Educational Psychology, Briefer Course," Teachers College, 1913. "Education," Macmillan, 1912.

Watson, J. B.: "Psychology from the Standpoint of a Behaviorist," Lippincott, 1918. "Behaviorism, Lectures-in-Print," People's Institute, 1925.

Wells, H. G.: "Floor Games," Small, Maynard and Co. "The Story of a Great Schoolmaster," Macmillan, 1924.

Woodrow H.: "Brightness and Dullness in Children," J. Lippincott.

Yeomans, Edward: "Shackled Youth," Atlantic Monthly Press, 1922.

United States Bureau of Education, bulletins and reports.

INDEX

A

ability, mental (*see also* mental testing)
abstractions, 80
abstract symbols, 30
academic work, 39; improves, 116, 148
activities, free, 95, 158
activity, adult conceived, 144
activities, constructive vs. destructive, 103; normal, 254
Adler, Felix, 126
age: grouping by chronological, 157; level, activities according to, 153, 157
America, 8, 63, 157
American Association of University Women, 54
American Child Health Organization, 54
American Federation of Teachers, 248
American Federation of Women's Clubs, 54
analytic psychology, 151, 157
anthropology, 4, 204
apathy, 14
arithmetic: in Dalton school, 91; in Pratt school, 154, 160 ff., 179 ff.; in work-study-play schools, 121; in Winnetka, 73; in vacuo, 16, 121
armories, 254
art, 157
assembly period, 39, 143
automatons, 147
authority, 114, 256

B

Baldwin, Bird T., 56, 59
Barrows, Alice, 108
Bassett, Rosa, 84
behavior disorders, 53
behavior psychology: applied to curriculum making, 132; study by Gesell, 56-58
Binet-Simon, 61
blocks, 6
book learning, discouraged, 149
Boston, 61, 92
Bourne, Randolph, 98, 99
bright children, 34
British, 83
Brookwood, 243
budget time, 45, 81
building, capacity increased, 108
Burk, Frederick, 82
Burris, W. P., 98

C

Caldwell, Otis W., 96, 134
California State Normal School, 82
Cane, Florence, 211 ff.
Chicago Board of Education, 118
child's level, 149, 254
child purposing, a régime of works, 44
Children's University School, 91
Children's School, 202
Child Welfare Research Station, 55

279